THE LADIES FOURSOME

ALSO BY NORM FOSTER

NORM FOSTER

THE LADIES FOURSOME

PLAYWRIGHTS CANADA PRESS
TORONTO

The Ladies Foursome © 2015 by Norm Foster

For professional or amateur production rights, please contact:
The GGA
250 The Esplanade, Suite 304
Toronto, ON M5A 1J2
416.928.0299, http://ggagency.ca/apply-for-performance-rights/

LIBRARY AND ARCHIVES CANADA CATALOGUING IN PUBLICATION
Foster, Norm, 1949-, author
        The ladies foursome / Norm Foster.

A play.
Issued in print and electronic formats.
ISBN 978-1-77091-426-1 (paperback).--ISBN 978-1-77091-427-8 (pdf).--
ISBN 978-1-77091-428-5 (epub).--ISBN 978-1-77091-429-2 (mobi)

        I. Title.

PS8561.O7745L33 2015   C812'.54   C2015-904085-X
                                                 C2015-904086-8

Playwrights Canada Press acknowledges that we operate on land which, for thousands of years, has been the traditional territories of the Mississaugas of the New Credit, the Huron-Wendat, the Anishinaabe, Métis, and the Haudenosaunee peoples. Today, this meeting place is still home to many Indigenous people from across Turtle Island and we are grateful to have the opportunity to work and play here.

We acknowledge the financial support of the Canada Council for the Arts—which last year invested $153 million to bring the arts to Canadians throughout the country—the Ontario Arts Council (OAC), Ontario Creates, and the Government of Canada for our publishing activities.

Canada Council   Conseil des arts
for the Arts   du Canada

ONTARIO ARTS COUNCIL
CONSEIL DES ARTS DE L'ONTARIO
an Ontario government agency
un organisme du gouvernement de l'Ontario

ONTARIO | ONTARIO
CREATES | CRÉATIF

The Ladies Foursome was first performed at the Upper Canada Playhouse in Morrisburg, Ontario, in July of 2014 with the following creative team:

Margot: Sharon Heldt
Tate: Leah Oster
Connie: Melanie Janzen
Dory: Jane Spence

Director: Jesse Collins
Stage manager: Jackie McCormick
Assistant stage manager: Sarah Barton
Set designer: Sean Free
Costume designer: Alex Amini

CHARACTERS

Margot: fifty to fifty-five years old
Tate: forty-two years old
Connie: fifty to fifty-five years old
Dory: around forty years old

TIME

A summer morning.

SETTING

A golf course. The set consists of tee blocks and a bench. The golfers can tee off in different directions each time, or they can tee off in the direction of the audience. They use imaginary tees and balls. Before each shot they will mime putting the tee in the ground and placing the ball on the tee. After the shot they will pick up the imaginary tee. Throughout the action Tate drinks from a Thermos.

ACT ONE

THE FIRST TEE

MARGOT and TATE enter with their golf clubs on pull carts. MARGOT is obviously hungover. She carries an unopened can of beer. TATE is a little perkier. She wears a pretty golf outfit. TATE starts doing stretches. MARGOT looks at her for a moment.

MARGOT: Shit.

TATE: What's wrong?

MARGOT: What is that you're doing there? What is that?

TATE: I'm stretching. You're supposed to get loose before you play. You should do it too.

MARGOT: Way ahead of you.

MARGOT opens the can of beer.

TATE: Margot, it's eight thirty in the morning.

MARGOT: Time. What is time? Time is just a way of letting us know what time it is.

TATE: Fine. I'm not your keeper. Do what you want.

MARGOT: I thank you for your blessing. Do you want one?

TATE: No, thanks. I've got my smoothie.

MARGOT: Well, I need something a little stronger. A little eye-opener.

TATE: What happened to Connie? I thought she was right behind us.

MARGOT: She stopped to talk to the cart kid.

TATE: The cart kid? The kid who brings the carts around?

MARGOT: Right. The cart kid.

TATE: Why is she talking to him? We're not getting carts.

MARGOT: I don't think she's talking to him about carts.

TATE: Oh, no. Really? Is there anybody she won't flirt with?

MARGOT: Oh, Tate, let her go. It makes her feel good. Makes her feel desirable.

TATE: Well, I think it's embarrassing. A woman her age.

MARGOT: She's my age.

TATE: Exactly. And where the heck is Dory? Our tee time is eight forty. I don't like people who are late. It's like they think their time is more valuable than mine.

MARGOT: She's not late. She's got nine minutes yet. And why are you being so judgmental this morning?

TATE: What do you mean, judgmental?

MARGOT: My drinking, Connie's flirting, Dory's almost-lateness.

TATE: I don't know. I guess the funeral yesterday has me re-evaluating things.

MARGOT: What things?

TATE: My life. Our lives.

MARGOT: You've got a great life.

TATE: All right, your lives. I mean, didn't Catherine's death make you think?

MARGOT: Sure it did.

TATE: And what did it make you think about? Did it make you think about not taking life for granted? About living each day to its fullest?

MARGOT: Catherine was struck by lightning while sitting at the top of a Ferris wheel. It made me think I should stay the hell away from carnivals.

TATE: Well, it made me think about a lot more than that. It made me think that I haven't made enough of this life I've been given. That I've frittered it away.

MARGOT: Frittered?

TATE: Frittered.

MARGOT: Like in a doughnut? That kind of frittered?

TATE: You know what I mean. I've squandered my life. It's been a life misspent.

MARGOT: Oh, what are you talking about? You've made a wonderful life for yourself. You've got a good man. Two beautiful children.

TATE: I've got three children.

MARGOT: I said beautiful. I'm kidding! I'm trying to lighten the mood here.

TATE: That's not funny.

MARGOT: I'm sorry.

TATE: That is not in the least bit funny, Margot.

MARGOT: I'm sorry. Tate, you're too young to have frittered away your life yet. You don't look back on a frittered-away life until you're in your sixties.

TATE: Which one is it?

MARGOT: Which one is what?

TATE: The child that isn't beautiful. It's Nigel, isn't it? Is it Nigel?

MARGOT: It's not Nigel.

TATE: We tried to have that lazy eye corrected. My God, he wore an eye patch until he was two. It was like breastfeeding Rooster Cogburn.

MARGOT: Tate, I was joking. Nigel is beautiful. They're all beautiful.

TATE: Do you mean that?

MARGOT: Yes.

TATE: You really mean that?

MARGOT: Yes. That lazy eye is adorable. Keeps people guessing. "Is he looking at me?"

CONNIE enters with her clubs on a pull cart.

CONNIE: That is one cute little piece of manhood. I'll tell you that for nothin'. Yes, ma'am, I'd give him a tumble.

TATE: He's half your age.

CONNIE: Then I'll give him two tumbles.

TATE: Connie, can I ask you something?

CONNIE: Sure.

TATE: What do you think of my kids?

CONNIE: What about your kids?

MARGOT: I said something as a joke and Tate took it the wrong way.

CONNIE: Oh, Tate, you can't take anything Margot says seriously. She's jaded. You've got two beautiful kids and Nigel. Be happy. So, where's the new girl? What's her name?

MARGOT: Dory. She's not here yet.

TATE: She's late.

MARGOT: She's not late. She's still got six minutes.

CONNIE: I was almost late myself. I had to drive all the way across town this morning to change.

MARGOT: All the way across town from where?

CONNIE: From this guy's place.

MARGOT: What guy? You met a guy?

CONNIE: I met a guy.

MARGOT: When?

CONNIE: Yesterday.

TATE: Yesterday? We were all at the funeral yesterday.

CONNIE: Yeah.

TATE: You met a guy at the funeral?

CONNIE: That's right.

TATE: You picked up a guy at the funeral, and you slept with him?

CONNIE: Gee, Tate, could that have sounded any more judgmental?

MARGOT: She's very judgmental this morning.

CONNIE: I'll say she is.

MARGOT: So, you picked up a guy at the funeral, and you slept with him?

CONNIE: Yep. But there was stuff in between. We didn't just go right from the gravesite to his kitchen table.

TATE: What stuff in between?

CONNIE: Well, driving. And we got some Chinese food. No, that was after. Or was it during? It was a kitchen table. I don't know what showed up when.

MARGOT: Which guy was it?

CONNIE: Ben.

TATE: Ben?

CONNIE: Yeah.

TATE: Ben Potter? Catherine's brother?

CONNIE: Right.

MARGOT: You slept with the deceased's brother?

CONNIE: Well, he looked like he could use some cheering up.

TATE: It was a funeral! We all needed cheering up.

CONNIE: Well, I couldn't sleep with everybody. Be sensible.

MARGOT: Wow, Connie, that's pretty fast work.

CONNIE: No, not really. Ben and I have always been attracted to each other. We both knew that. And then when we saw each other yesterday, you know.

MARGOT: Grief and a mutual sense of loss drove you into each other's arms?

CONNIE: I was going to say we got horny, but let's go with yours.

TATE: Connie, don't you ever worry about getting a reputation?

CONNIE: Oh, sweetie, at my age I don't worry about getting a reputation. I worry about keeping it.

TATE: But what about your public image?

CONNIE: Tate, come on. I see the news on television. A woman can't win in that job anyway. People think I'm there either because I'm eye candy or because I'm a bitch.

MARGOT: And which one are you?

CONNIE: I'm neither. I'm there because I'm good at what I do. The fact that I'm eye candy too is just gravy. Woo! Up top!

CONNIE and MARGOT high-five. DORY enters pulling her clubs on a pull cart.

DORY: Good morning.

CONNIE: Oh, there she is.

MARGOT: Hi, Dory.

DORY: Hi. Boy, I just made it. I was leaving the hotel when my husband called, and he put the kids on and I had to talk to all of them.

CONNIE: How many kids have you got?

DORY: Six.

CONNIE: Six? Wow. Catholic?

DORY: Careless. But I'm here now. Rental clubs and all. I don't know how good I'll be without my own clubs and golf shoes. I hope I don't hold you up.

MARGOT: You'll be fine. Do you golf much?

DORY: Not as much as I'd like to. Summer is our busy time. We own a lodge up on Arrowhead Lake, and that and the kids really keep us hopping.

MARGOT: Do you live up there year-round?

DORY: Yep. We love it up there. I guess we're country folk at heart. Little country mice. We sit out on the porch at night and look up at those stars and hear nothing but the breeze in the treetops, and we wonder how anyone could live anywhere else.

CONNIE: I prefer the city. I need that ambient noise outside. Makes me feel like I'm part of something.

MARGOT: Yeah. A crime scene.

DORY: Listen, thanks for inviting me today. I think it's lovely that you decided to play a round of golf in honour of Cathy. She would have liked that. You all played once a week together, right?

MARGOT: Weather permitting. We've done it for the last fourteen years.

DORY: I think that's wonderful.

TATE: You called her "Cathy"?

DORY: Uh-huh.

TATE: I thought she didn't like "Cathy."

CONNIE: She hated "Cathy."

DORY: Well, that's what I called her. I called her that the whole time I knew her.

MARGOT: How long was that?

DORY: She started coming up to the lodge twelve years ago. She spent two weeks up there every summer, relaxing, taking photographs.

MARGOT: She told us she went to a lodge every summer. Didn't tell us much about it though.

TATE: Okay, that group ahead of us is out of range. Who wants to go first?

CONNIE: Let our guest go first. Is that okay with you?

DORY: Sure. This is going to be fun. We'll get to spend a few hours together. I'll get to know you gals better. I mean, I've heard so much about you from Cathy over the years. And now here you are, in the flesh. Okay. Here we go.

She tees her ball and lines up her shot, and then steps back and lines up her shot some more.

Cathy and I golfed together once in a while. I don't know if she told you that. We'd play once or twice when she visited. She was always asking me for help on her putting. She wasn't a very good putter. Not to speak ill of the dead.

She steps up to her ball and then steps back from the ball again.

I think it was because she had trouble lining up her putts. One eye was out of sync with the other. But not a lazy eye. God, no. Not that gross. Okay. This is it.

She steps up then steps back again.

Oh, wait. Because we're playing this round for Cathy, maybe someone should say something first.

MARGOT: Say what?

DORY: Some words.

CONNIE: You mean, like, hit the damn ball? Those words?

DORY: No, I mean some words about Cathy. Shouldn't one of us say something? Tate?

TATE: No, I'm not very good at that. I don't know any prayers.

CONNIE: I'm afraid if I start to pray I might be the second lightning casualty.

DORY: It doesn't have to be a prayer. Just some nice words.

Nobody says anything.

DORY: All right, then; I'll say something. Uh . . . let's see. Cathy?

TATE: Should we bow our heads?

CONNIE: She said it wasn't a prayer.

(to DORY) It's not a prayer, right?

DORY: No.

TATE: So, we don't bow our heads?

DORY: I suppose you don't need to.

TATE: What about hats? Do we take off our hats?

CONNIE: You're wearing a visor.

TATE: Well, a visor's a hat.

CONNIE: A visor's a visor.

TATE: So I should leave it on? Dory, should I leave it on?

DORY: I'm not sure.

TATE: If you're going to say religious words I should probably take it off. Are you going to say religious words?

DORY: I'm not sure what words I'm going to say.

MARGOT: Aw, hell, I'll say the words. Catherine, you went to the fair and now you're dead, so now we're golfing with Dory instead. Cheers.

MARGOT takes a drink. The other three stare at her.

What? I want to play golf.

TATE: That wasn't very respectful.

MARGOT: Never mind. Dory, hit the ball.

DORY hits the ball.

Nice one.

DORY: Thank you.

TATE: You could have said something with more feeling.

MARGOT: I'm all out of feeling. Connie, you're next.

CONNIE tees up her ball.

TATE: What do you mean you're out of feeling?

MARGOT: Look, we cried all day yesterday, right?

CONNIE: Well, not all day.

MARGOT: All right, some of us cried; some of us moaned. Well, now it's time to celebrate Catherine's life. Not cry about it.

CONNIE hits her ball.

DORY: Beautiful.

CONNIE: It'll do.

MARGOT: All right, Tate, you're up.

TATE: I just think the mood should be a little more sombre, that's all.

MARGOT: We're playing golf. We'll all be sombre soon enough.

DORY: I think Margot's right. I think Cathy would want us to enjoy ourselves today and remember her fondly.

TATE: I just don't want her to think that we've moved on from our grief too quickly.

MARGOT: She's gone. She's not thinking anything. Now hit the ball.

TATE tees off. MARGOT tees up her ball.

TATE: It still seems a little cold to me.

MARGOT: I'm sorry. I just don't like to dwell on the negative. We've all had tragedy in our lives, and Catherine's death was a great tragedy. We deal with it and we move on. We don't let the heartbreak consume us.

MARGOT hits her ball.

Shit!

They all grab their carts and begin to exit.

CONNIE: Now, that was real heartbreaking, that was. But that's okay, Margot. Don't dwell on it. Just deal with it and move on.

DORY: Okay, we're off. Let the games begin.

DORY and TATE exit.

CONNIE: Six kids. God, even I say no once in a while.

MARGOT and CONNIE exit.

THE SECOND TEE

They enter. CONNIE is marking the score on the scorecard.

DORY: Cathy was great with my kids. They loved her. She would have made a wonderful mother.

TATE: So, six children, huh?

DORY: That's right.

TATE: Are they all beautiful?

DORY: They sure are.

TATE: All of them? I mean, you don't have one that might be a little less beautiful? Average even?

DORY: Oh, no. As parents, we find all of our children beautiful, right?

TATE: Uh-huh.

CONNIE: The birdie gets the honour.

MARGOT: Yes, that was a nice putt, Dory.

DORY: I got lucky.

CONNIE: Well don't expect that to continue. This is a pretty tough course.

MARGOT: So, is Dory short for something?

DORY: Doris. I was named after my grandmother on my mother's side. But my father didn't like "Doris," so he called me "Dory."

MARGOT: I don't mind "Doris."

DORY: No, not the name. My father didn't like Doris my grandmother.

DORY tees off.

TATE: Wow, another nice shot.

MARGOT: Beautiful.

DORY: Thanks.

CONNIE tees up the ball for her shot.

MARGOT: How long have you been a golfer?

DORY: Quite a while. My father taught me how to play. We used to hit balls in the field behind our house. What about you?

MARGOT: I started when Connie and Catherine asked me to join them for a game fourteen years ago.

DORY: And you liked it right away?

MARGOT: I hated it. I still hate it. But where else can you drink this early in the morning and have people think it's normal?

DORY: What about you, Tate? How did you get started?

TATE: I started because of my husband.

CONNIE hits her ball.

DORY: Very nice shot. Your husband?

TATE tees up her ball.

TATE: Yeah. Bobby was always trying to get me to play golf, and I was always trying to get him to go scuba diving, one of my passions. He said, "If God wanted me to go underwater he would have given me gills." And I said, "If God wanted me to golf he would have given me balls." So, we made an agreement. I'd try golf, and he'd try scuba diving. I liked golf, and he almost drowned.

TATE hits her ball.

DORY: Ooh, you got all of that one.

MARGOT tees up her ball.

CONNIE: You didn't ask me how long I've been playing.

DORY: Oh, I can tell you've been playing for a long, long, long time.

CONNIE: Really?

DORY: Long time.

CONNIE: How old do you think I am, anyway?

DORY: No, I didn't mean because of your age. I meant because of your prowess. I mean, you don't hit a shot like you just hit unless you've been playing for a long, long, long time.

CONNIE: Uh-huh.

DORY: Many, many, many years.

CONNIE: *(to MARGOT)* What are you waiting for?

MARGOT: Nothing. Just enjoying the moment.

MARGOT hits her ball.

Shit.

CONNIE: That's all right. You're only a chainsaw away from the fairway.

DORY: So, do you girls ever play for money?

TATE: Play what for money? Golf?

DORY: Yeah.

TATE: No, this is just a friendly game.

DORY: Oh. Okay.

CONNIE: Why? Do you want to play for money?

DORY: No, no. It's just that sometimes it makes it more interesting. But no, we're here to golf in the name of Cathy. A wager would sully that.

CONNIE: No, no, wait. You would want to play for money? I mean, someone who wants to play for money usually thinks they can win. Do you think you can win?

DORY: Well . . .

MARGOT: What Connie means is do you think you can beat her?

CONNIE: *(to MARGOT)* No, that's not what I mean.

(to DORY) But is that what you think?

DORY: Well, what's the score after one hole?

TATE: You're up by one stroke.

MARGOT: Dory's up by one stroke.

DORY: I'm up by one stroke.

CONNIE: All right, let's play for money then.

TATE: No way. No. Margot and I aren't in your class. We wouldn't stand a chance.

MARGOT: Tate's right. Besides, I don't come here to bet on golf. I come here to drink.

CONNIE: We'll play teams then. Best ball. Each team takes the better shot of the two and you play from there.

DORY: How much are we playing for?

CONNIE: Dollar a hole?

DORY: Well, that's fine, but you know one team wins a hole, the other teams wins a hole. It doesn't add up. You wind up winning two or three dollars in total.

CONNIE: Well, how much do you want to play for?

DORY: Why not just a lump sum? We each throw some money in the pot and the winning team splits it at the end.

TATE: How much money?

DORY: Five hundred dollars each?

TATE: Five hundred? I don't have five hundred dollars! Where am I going to get five hundred dollars?

CONNIE: Your husband's a surgeon.

TATE: Oh, that's right. I'm rich. Yay!

CONNIE: All right, five hundred dollars it is.

MARGOT: What will the teams be?

CONNIE: Well, Doris and I will be on opposite teams because she obviously thinks she can beat me.

DORY: No, I didn't say that. I don't even have my own clubs.

CONNIE: Right, the rental clubs. Well, that does put you at a disadvantage.

TATE: I'll play with Connie.

TATE moves to CONNIE's side.

MARGOT: No, I'll play with Connie.

MARGOT moves to CONNIE's side.

TATE: I called it first.

MARGOT: We don't call. There's no calling. What is this, high school?

CONNIE: Ladies, did it ever occur to you that a display like this might hurt our guest's feelings?

TATE: You're right. I'm sorry, Dory. That was thoughtless.

MARGOT: I'm sorry too.

DORY: No, it's fine.

CONNIE: I mean, sure, she doesn't play very much, and she hasn't got her own clubs, and she was taught by her father in some farmer's field in Saskatchewan.

DORY: Arizona.

CONNIE: Pardon me?

DORY: Arizona. That's where I grew up. That's where my father taught me how to play. Of course he didn't have much time for lessons. He was on the road most of the year.

MARGOT: Oh? What did he do?

DORY: He was on the tour.

CONNIE: What tour?

DORY: The PGA Tour. David Lakeside. Maybe you've heard of him.

TATE: What's the PGA Tour?

CONNIE: The Professional Golfers Association Tour. Your father was David Lakeside?

DORY: Is David Lakeside. That's right.

CONNIE: He won the Canadian Open.

DORY: Twice.

MARGOT and TATE both scramble to stand beside DORY. They each grab an arm.

TATE: I'll play with Dory.

MARGOT: No, I will.

TATE: I had her first.

MARGOT: No, you didn't!

TATE: Did too!

CONNIE: Ladies. Did it ever occur to you that a display like this might hurt my feelings?

MARGOT: No.

TATE: No.

CONNIE: Tate, you're on my team.

TATE: Why?

CONNIE: Because you're the weak one and I'm cutting you from the herd. Now let's go.

MARGOT: Wait a minute. Wait. Let's not play for money. It's already changing the complexion of the game, and not for the better. Let's just play for lunch.

CONNIE: Lunch?

MARGOT: Yeah. The losing team buys the winning team lunch after the match.

CONNIE: All right. I'll go for that.

TATE: That sounds very civilized.

MARGOT: Dory? How's that sound to you?

Beat.

DORY: Good. Fine. Lunch it is.

CONNIE: And it starts right now. On this hole. The last one doesn't count, right?

MARGOT: Right.

CONNIE: Good. Come on, Tate. I'm counting on you for the short game.

TATE: What's that?

CONNIE: The short game. Putting, chipping.

TATE: Oh.

CONNIE: You've played with us for fourteen years and you don't know what the short game is?

TATE: How would I know that? We don't talk about golf out here. We talk about everything but golf.

MARGOT: She's right.

CONNIE: Damn. She is right. Well, pull it together, because today we focus on golf.

TATE: Are we going to lose?

CONNIE: No, we're not.

TATE: What's chipping?

CONNIE and TATE exit.

DORY: Connie seems kind of competitive.

MARGOT: Oh, she's competitive all right.

DORY: What happens when she loses?

MARGOT: I don't know. She's never lost.

DORY: What?

MARGOT: Not once. The whole time we've been playing, Tate or I or Catherine, for that matter, have never scored better than Connie.

DORY: That's quite the streak.

MARGOT: It sure is. Fourteen years.

DORY: Wow. Maybe I should let her win then.

MARGOT: What do you mean?

DORY: Well, if she's that used to winning, and you're used to losing, maybe we should just keep everything status quo. Why upset the apple cart?

MARGOT: I never thought about that. That's probably a good idea. But no. Kick her ass.

MARGOT exits. DORY follows.

THE THIRD TEE

They enter.

TATE: It's just that some parents can look at their children and objectively say, "Well, this one isn't quite as adorable as this one." Or, "This one's got that thing that makes him funny-looking."

DORY: What thing?

TATE: Anything. A mole. A crooked nose. Anything at all.

DORY: Nope. I see the beauty in each of my children. It might not be on the surface, but it's there.

TATE: Ah-hah!

DORY: Ah-hah what?

TATE: So you do have one of those.

DORY: One of those what?

TATE: One of those children that has a thing that makes him . . .

DORY: Makes him what?

TATE: You know? Homely.

DORY: Homely?

TATE: Oh, God. I'm an awful mother!

MARGOT: Oh, Tate, cut it out.

TATE: I am. That child came out of me and I talk about him like that. Shame on me. I should wash my uterus out with soap.

CONNIE: Your mouth. You should wash your mouth out with soap.

TATE: What did I say?

CONNIE: Your uterus.

TATE: Oh my God! That must have been Freudian.

DORY: I don't understand.

MARGOT: Tate has a son named Nigel, and he's got a lazy eye.

DORY: Ohhh.

CONNIE: Listen, the kid's name is Nigel. I think the lazy eye is the least of his worries.

TATE: It was Bobby's grandfather's name.

CONNIE: Doris, you're away again.

DORY: No, that group ahead of us is still in range.

CONNIE: You think you can hit the ball that far?

DORY: I might.

CONNIE: And while we're on the subject of names, isn't "Bobby" a little weird for a grown man?

TATE: What do you mean?

CONNIE: Bobby. He's a surgeon. He should call himself "Robert." It's more dignified.

TATE: He's a *vascular* surgeon. He's very particular about that.

CONNIE: Oh sure, he's particular about *that* name, but he's okay with "Bobby."

TATE: What's wrong with "Bobby"?

CONNIE: It's not grown-up. Uh, Bobby, we're replacing a heart valve here. Can you put down the Lego?

(to DORY) Doris, hit the ball. They're way out of your range.

DORY tees up her ball.

TATE: Well, I like "Bobby." It's carefree. It's not stuffy.

CONNIE: It's immature.

TATE: It's not immature.

CONNIE: And it doesn't have distinction. I mean, can you think of one famous man named "Bobby"? Huh? One? No. I rest my case.

DORY hits her ball. The four of them stare at the ball as it goes.

DORY: Oh my God!

CONNIE: You should have waited.

DORY: Oh my God. Did I hit him?

CONNIE: You sure did.

TATE: You should have yelled "fore."

DORY: I should have, shouldn't I? Fore!

MARGOT: It's a little late now. Saying it now is just mocking the poor bugger.

DORY: Oh my God.

CONNIE: Don't worry about it.

DORY: Don't worry about it? Look!

DORY points out onto the golf course.

CONNIE: It's okay. He's back on his feet again. Wait, no. He's down again. Oh, there we go. He's up.

(yelling out) Walk it off!

He's fine.

MARGOT: You're next, Connie.

CONNIE: I think I'll wait.

TATE: Well, now that we've got a few minutes until the paramedics arrive, tell me this, Dory. How did you wind up going from Arizona to an isolated place like Arrowhead Lake?

DORY: Oh, uh, I don't know. Love, I guess. Following my husband's dream.

(looking down the fairway) Do you really think he's all right?

CONNIE: Yeah, they've dragged his lifeless carcass back onto the cart.

TATE: You didn't have dreams of your own?

DORY: Pardon me?

TATE: You said you were following your husband's dream. You didn't have any dreams of your own?

DORY: Oh, at one time I did.

MARGOT: And you, what, put them on hold for your husband?

DORY: Well, kind of, I guess. They weren't big dreams anyway, so it didn't matter.

TATE: Any dream should matter. Big or small.

DORY: No, it was fine. It was the right thing to do. But I want to find out more about you three. You own a construction company, Margot?

MARGOT: How'd you know that?

DORY: Cathy told me. We talked about you three a lot.

MARGOT: Oh. Yeah, I took over the company when my father died. I didn't plan on making it my life's work, but I had a knack for it, I guess, so here I am. But I love it. It's very challenging, and I get to tell men what to do.

CONNIE: I love doing that too. Oh, you mean in the workplace.

DORY: How old were you when you took over?

MARGOT: Twenty-five.

DORY: Wow. That's young. How did the men feel about having a twenty-five-year-old woman for a boss?

MARGOT: They didn't care for it at first. Until they saw that I knew what I was doing.

DORY: Did your father teach you the business?

MARGOT: Yeah. I used to go to work with him all the time when I was a little girl. It was the only way I got to see him. The business took up most of his time.

DORY: And it doesn't take up most of yours?

MARGOT: Connie, they're out of range now.

CONNIE *tees up the ball for her shot.*

DORY: Margot? The business doesn't take up most of your time?

CONNIE: That's kind of a sensitive area, Doris.

DORY: Oh. Sorry.

MARGOT: No, that's okay. Yes, it takes up most of my time. It takes up all of my time. It's cost me a husband and a daughter. I didn't have time to make my marriage work, and I didn't spend enough time with my daughter, so I lost them both. And as a result, in the words of Mr. Bojangles, I drinks a bit. But I've got a thriving business, and that's the main thing, right? That's what I've worked hard for all these years.

CONNIE: Well, that was a shameless outpouring of self-pity.

MARGOT: Shut up.

CONNIE: Hey, I didn't ask the question. Dottie did.

CONNIE *hits her shot.*

TATE: Good one, Connie! Yes!

TATE *tees up her shot.*

DORY: How old is your daughter?

MARGOT: Twenty-five.

DORY: Where is she?

MARGOT: She lives here.

DORY: What does she do?

MARGOT: She was just called to the bar.

DORY: Oh, a lawyer. Impressive. Was it a nice ceremony?

MARGOT: I hear it was, yes.

TATE hits her ball.

CONNIE: Good girl!

DORY: And you're a stay-at-home mom, Tate?

TATE: Uh-huh.

DORY: Yeah, me too. Well, along with running the lodge.

MARGOT tees up her ball.

How old are your children?

TATE: Sixteen, fourteen, and thirteen.

DORY: Three teenagers.

TATE: Right. The first sign of the apocalypse. How old are yours?

DORY: My oldest is twelve.

TATE: And the rest?

DORY: The rest are just a blur. They were coming out so fast I felt like the ball machine in a batting cage.

MARGOT: So, you have six kids, and the oldest is twelve. So you've had a baby every two years.

DORY: That's right. After the last one I wondered if these legs were ever to going to close again. That's when I insisted that my husband get a vasectomy.

CONNIE: How did your husband feel about that?

DORY: Not too thrilled. Men are such babies about that part of their anatomy.

MARGOT: Well, I think it depends on if you're going down there with good intentions or not. They don't want anyone taking sharp implements down there.

CONNIE: It's a good bargaining tool though. Pardon the pun.

TATE: Bargaining tool how?

CONNIE: Well, if you want something badly enough and your husband is digging his heels in, you just tell him the vacation is off.

TATE: What vacation?

CONNIE: You know? You won't be going south.

They all stop and think about this. Then they get it.

DORY: Oh, no. I would never do that. That's using sex as leverage. That's an awful thing to do.

MARGOT: Dory's right. That cheapens a woman, Connie.

TATE: It wouldn't work for me anyway.

CONNIE and DORY look at TATE. MARGOT hits her ball.

MARGOT: Shit!

TATE: Okay, here we go.

TATE begins to move.

CONNIE: Wait, wait. What do you mean, it wouldn't work for you?

TATE: It just wouldn't. Bobby doesn't put that high a value on sex.

TATE begins to leave.

CONNIE: Wait, wait, wait. What do you mean? You mean he doesn't enjoy it?

TATE: No, I didn't say he didn't enjoy it. It's just not a priority in our marriage.

MARGOT: So you don't do it a lot?

TATE: I didn't say that.

CONNIE: You're telling us this now? We've played together for fourteen years and only now you're telling us your sex life is in a shambles? We could have been joking about this for years!

TATE: My sex life is not in a shambles. My sex life is fine.

MARGOT: Fine? Just fine? That's not good.

DORY: Definitely not good.

CONNIE: And Doris is an expert. Apparently she and her husband have sex at the drop of a . . . well, whenever she drops something. You see? You see what I've been missing out on?

TATE: Our sex life is healthy. Thank you.

MARGOT: What's healthy to you? How many times a week?

TATE: I don't know. Once?

CONNIE: Once?

TATE: In a good week.

CONNIE: That's not healthy. That's malnourished.

MARGOT: It's sickly.

CONNIE: It's on life support.

TATE: Now, wait a minute. You two don't even have men. You can't judge how healthy once a week is in a marriage.

DORY: I think she might have a point there, ladies.

CONNIE: We've both been married. We can base it on that. And Vic and I used to do it four times a week on average.

MARGOT: Larry and I only did it once a week.

TATE: You see?

MARGOT: Then four times a week after we got divorced.

CONNIE: So what's the problem with you and Bobby?

TATE: There is no problem.

MARGOT: Do *you* enjoy it? Is it good for *you*?

TATE: Sure. For the most part.

MARGOT: Tate?

TATE: Well, it's just that he's a doctor. The sex is very clinical. It's like he does this, and then I do that, and then he does this, and I do that, and then he does this, and I fake that.

CONNIE: Does he ever do . . . that?

TATE: That? Oh, yeah. He does that sometimes. In fact, when he does that, I don't have to fake that.

TATE exits.

CONNIE: I hear that.

The other three exit.

THE FOURTH TEE

They enter. MARGOT *does not have a beer in her hand.*

DORY: Sorry about that, Margot.

MARGOT: Don't worry about it. It was a tough putt.

CONNIE: And it puts us up by one stroke. Okay, this is a par five, Doris. And there's water at about a hundred and ninety yards.

CONNIE *tees up her ball.*

DORY: Got it. Oh, guess who I saw on the way over here this morning. Cathy's brother, Ben.

TATE: Really?

DORY: I was at a stoplight, and I looked over, and there he was in the car beside me. He seemed to be in good spirits too. In fact, almost too good. He was singing along to the radio, playing the air drums. He seemed quite happy.

MARGOT: Well, some people overcome grief in different ways.

CONNIE: So, Doris, I'm curious.

DORY: Yes?

CONNIE: Well, on the last tee you asked about Tate's employment situation—stay-at-home mom.

TATE: Because I'm rich. Yay.

CONNIE: And you mentioned Margot's construction business.

DORY: Yes, I'm very impressed by that. A woman running a construction company? Very impressed.

MARGOT: Thank you.

CONNIE: Yeah, that's lovely. But you didn't ask about me.

TATE: Are you feeling left out, Connie?

CONNIE: No. It just seems odd to me that you wouldn't want to know what I do for a living.

DORY: Oh, I know what you do for a living.

CONNIE: You do?

DORY: Of course. I mean, who doesn't know Connie Sajack? The region's best news anchor.

CONNIE: Well, I don't know if I'm the best.

DORY: That's what your ads say. "Connie Sajack. The region's best news anchor." Isn't that what they say?

CONNIE: Yes, that's what they say.

DORY: And they wouldn't lie, would they? I mean, it's television. They wouldn't say you're the best if you weren't, right?

CONNIE: Well . . .

DORY: But who determines who's the best? That's what I wonder. Is it a competition? Is it voted on? If it is, well, congratulations, missy. That's a big honour.

CONNIE: Thank you.

MARGOT: Okay, quiet everybody. Connie's teeing off. Connie Sajack! The region's best news anchor.

CONNIE hits her ball. They all watch.

Soon to be the region's wettest news anchor.

TATE: *(teeing up her ball)* So, how *do* they determine that, Connie? Who the best anchor is, I mean.

CONNIE: It's just a promotional ad, Tate. It doesn't mean anything.

TATE: So you're not the region's best news anchor? I mean, they shouldn't be able to say that if you're not. That's false advertising.

CONNIE: Well, maybe I am the region's best news anchor.

TATE: The ads don't say "maybe." The ads say you *are* the region's best news anchor.

CONNIE: Just hit your ball, would you?

TATE tees off.

TATE: Oooh, that's not bad.

DORY tees up her ball.

DORY: I'm sorry, Connie. I didn't mean to open up a can of worms.

CONNIE: It's fine.

DORY: I mean, I don't know who's the best. I never watch you, so I can't judge.

CONNIE: Of course. I guess you don't get us way up there on Arrowhead Lake.

DORY: No, we get you.

DORY *hits her ball.*

MARGOT: Great shot, Dory.

DORY: It wasn't that great.

MARGOT: No, I meant the shot you just took at Connie.

MARGOT *tees up her ball.*

TATE: Well, I think you're the best, Connie. Bobby and I watch you in bed every night.

CONNIE: Thanks, Tate. Now I'll be picturing you and Bobby in bed while I'm reading the news. Thanks a lot.

TATE: What's wrong with that?

MARGOT: Yeah, it's not like they're having sex while they're watching.

DORY: Once a week they are.

MARGOT: You'll just have to guess which night that is.

TATE: Friday.

MARGOT hits her ball.

MARGOT: Shit!

DORY: So, how did you get into television?

CONNIE: I studied journalism in university. I was a reporter overseas for a while working with my husband—he was a cameraman—and then . . . and then I got offered the anchor job, and I took it.

DORY: Oh. Good. So now I know everything about your employment situation too. You don't have to feel left out anymore. Okay, here's where we make our move, Margot.

TATE and DORY exit.

CONNIE: How much do you think she knows about us?

MARGOT: Why?

CONNIE: Well, she knew Catherine for twelve years, and she says Catherine talked about us.

MARGOT: So?

CONNIE: So, wouldn't Catherine have told her what happened?

MARGOT: I don't know. Maybe not.

CONNIE: I'm just wondering how many of these questions are genuine and how many are trying to catch us in lies.

MARGOT: Why would she want to catch us in lies?

CONNIE: I don't know. I haven't thought that far ahead.

MARGOT: No, I think she's genuinely interested in getting to know us better. She feels that we have a common bond in Catherine, and she wants us all to be friends.

CONNIE: Maybe.

MARGOT: I'm sure of it.

CONNIE: We'll see.

CONNIE begins to exit.

MARGOT: And I think she genuinely wants to know who decided you were the region's best news anchor.

CONNIE: Never mind.

CONNIE exits.

MARGOT: I'd like to know too, missy.

MARGOT exits.

THE FIFTH TEE

They enter. They will all use irons on this tee.

DORY: So finally, last year, my husband and I decided we should sit down with our two oldest girls and talk about the facts of life.

TATE: And how did that go?

DORY: Good. We learned quite a bit.

CONNIE: Doris, you're up.

MARGOT: Yes, way to go, Dory. You've got us all even again.

DORY: *(teeing up her ball)* It wasn't just me, Margot. You hit a great second shot.

MARGOT: But you hit that gorgeous approach shot.

DORY: And then you got us close with that chip.

MARGOT: And your putt was a thing of beauty.

CONNIE: Would you two like some alone time?

DORY: All right. A little par three. Let's put it on the dance floor.

DORY hits her ball.

There we go.

MARGOT tees up her ball.

TATE: I wonder why Catherine never told us about you, Dory. I mean, she went up to your lodge every year. You played golf with her. I'm surprised she never mentioned you.

DORY: Well, Cathy struck me as kind of a private person. Maybe she wanted to keep those trips to herself.

TATE: But we were her best friends. Why would she want to keep it from us?

MARGOT hits her ball.

MARGOT: Shit! I guess we'll be using your shot, Dory.

CONNIE: Maybe she was rendezvousing with a man up there. Is that it, Doris? Was Catherine shtupping a guy on these trips?

TATE: Oh, geez, Connie.

CONNIE: What?

TATE: "Shtupping"?

CONNIE: What's wrong with "shtupping"?

TATE: It's tasteless.

CONNIE: Oh, you're such a prude.

CONNIE tees up her ball.

TATE: I am not a prude. I just think the act of lovemaking should be referred to with more reverence. It's a very personal encounter. The most intimate interaction two people can have together, and I think it should be given the respect it's due.

CONNIE: Fine. So, Doris, was Catherine playing hide the knack-wurst with some guy?

CONNIE hits her shot.

Well?

TATE tees up her ball.

MARGOT: I don't think it's any of our business what Catherine was doing up there. If she wanted to keep it a secret, she must have had a good reason. Or maybe there was no reason. Maybe there was nothing to tell. She went up to Arrowhead Lake for a couple of weeks each summer. That was it. Nothing more.

TATE: Maybe.

TATE hits her shot.

CONNIE: That's my partner.

TATE: She was kind of quiet anyway, right? A schoolteacher. Never made any waves.

MARGOT: Always on an even keel. Everyone liked her.

TATE: There was never any drama in her life.

CONNIE: She never went through a divorce. Never had family problems.

MARGOT: And she never had to worry about money after she won the lottery.

DORY: What? Cathy won the lottery?

CONNIE: Five years ago.

MARGOT: Half a million dollars.

DORY: Wow. She didn't tell me about that.

CONNIE: And it was the first time she'd ever bought a ticket.

DORY: Really?

CONNIE: Yep.

DORY: Wow.

TATE: Yeah, Catherine always was the lucky one.

The other three stare at TATE.

Well, apart from the lightning strike.

CONNIE: *(to DORY)* So, she didn't tell you about her lottery win?

DORY: No. Didn't say a word.

CONNIE: Hmm. And she didn't tell us about you. Strange.

TATE: It's like she was leading a double life.

MARGOT: Well, I wouldn't go that far. She had some secrets. So what? Everybody's got secrets.

DORY: Margot's right. We're here to celebrate Cathy. Not to cast aspersions.

CONNIE: *(to MARGOT)* What secrets do you have?

MARGOT: What?

CONNIE: You said everybody's got secrets. So, what secrets do you have?

MARGOT: I wasn't talking about me in particular. I was talking about people in general. As a whole. As a whole, we have secrets.

CONNIE: Oh my God.

MARGOT: What?

CONNIE: You do have a secret.

MARGOT: No, I don't.

CONNIE: You do! She does have a secret.

TATE: Do you, Margot?

MARGOT: No.

TATE: Margot, come on. I'm a stay-at-home mom staring at a lazy eye all day and sleeping with a man who doesn't give a sweet fig about sex. Now throw me a bone!

MARGOT: All right, I've got a little secret.

TATE: That's better. What is it?

MARGOT: It's nothing. I'm . . . I'm seeing somebody. That's all.

CONNIE: Seeing somebody? You mean a man?

MARGOT: Yes, a man.

TATE: Romantically?

MARGOT: Very much so.

CONNIE: Well, bend me over and call me Spanky.

MARGOT: Is that so hard to believe?

CONNIE: No. I'm very happy for you.

DORY: Congratulations, Margot. I think it's wonderful.

MARGOT: Thank you, Dory.

TATE: So, who is it?

MARGOT: Just a guy I met through work.

TATE: A construction guy?

CONNIE: Does he wear a tool belt? I love tool belts. All that stuff that's on there. Like the ball-peen hammer and the screwdriver. And they all jiggle when he walks.

MARGOT: He's not a construction guy. He owns property downtown. We're doing a job for him.

TATE: Oh, a property owner. Nice.

DORY: How long have you been seeing him?

MARGOT: Not long. About a month.

CONNIE: And now for the big question.

MARGOT: What's that?

CONNIE: Have you, uh . . . you know?

MARGOT: Have I what?

TATE: Shtupped him?

MARGOT: I'm not going to answer that. That's personal.

CONNIE: So you have.

MARGOT: I said I'm not answering that.

CONNIE: So you haven't.

MARGOT: Connie!

CONNIE: She does have a glow on. Do you see that glow?

TATE: That could be the three beers.

DORY: That's okay, Margot. You keep that information to yourself.

MARGOT: I will. I'll keep it entirely to myself. It's nobody's business but my own that I'm having the best sex I've ever had in my entire freaking life!

MARGOT exits.

TATE: I wonder when I'm going to have the best sex of my entire freaking life.

CONNIE: Maybe you already are.

CONNIE and DORY exit.

TATE: Shit.

TATE exits.

THE SIXTH TEE

They enter.

CONNIE: I think my underwear's on backwards. Do you ever get that feeling? It's like I'm walking one way, and my underwear's walking in an entirely different direction.

TATE: That's what happens when you dress in the aftermath of passion.

CONNIE: Well, you would know. Once a week.

CONNIE marks the scorecard.

Okay, we tied that hole.

(to DORY) Gidget, you're up.

DORY tees her ball.

TATE: Do you guys believe in life after death?

DORY: Yes.

CONNIE: No.

MARGOT: Maybe.

CONNIE: No, I think if you start to believe in life after death, then you won't make the best of this life because you figure you're getting another chance later on. This is it, girls. Your one shot. You've got to live in the here and now.

MARGOT: The older I get, the more I want to believe in it. It's like Connie says. I want another chance at life because I haven't done so well with this one.

CONNIE: You've done fine with this one. You've built up a good business. You've got a new man.

MARGOT: But I've failed in a couple of very important areas. Plus, I don't like the finality of death. That's an awful thought.

DORY hits her ball.

TATE: Nice.

MARGOT tees up her ball.

DORY: Don't worry, Margot. You'll be fine. The Bible says when we die our body returns to dust and our spirit returns to God in a conscious state awaiting judgment. Then all of the dead, good and bad, are made immortal, after which they will either enter heaven, or if they have sinned, will suffer eternal damnation and burn forever in the fires of hell.

CONNIE: Why is she looking at me?

TATE: I'm just asking because of Catherine. It's not fair that her life was cut short like that. I hope she's enjoying a new life somewhere else.

MARGOT hits her ball.

MARGOT: That's better!

DORY: Don't worry, Tate. Cathy is one of the good ones. I'm sure she's in heaven as we speak.

CONNIE tees up her ball.

CONNIE: Are you a believer, Doris?

DORY: In God? Yes, I am.

CONNIE: Well, I've seen enough over the years to make me a doubter. If there is a God, he or she has dropped the ball more than just a few times.

DORY: You see, that's the common misconception. God isn't here to save us when we're in danger, or to cure our disease, or to lift us up out of poverty or despair. No, God is here as a teacher. A guide. If you believe in Him, you will follow His teachings, and you will lift yourself up. It's that simple.

TATE: You think God is a man?

DORY: I think God is man and woman. God is all of us.

CONNIE: Well, if there is a God, he's a man.

MARGOT: What makes you say that?

CONNIE: Well, the Bible says that God rested on the seventh day. A woman wouldn't rest on the seventh day. No, she'd say, "I'm going to organize that closet."

CONNIE tees off. TATE tees up her ball.

TATE: Well, I hope you're right, Dory. I hope Catherine is looking down on us from heaven right now with God on one side of her and Gregory Peck on the other.

MARGOT: *(to DORY)* Catherine always had a thing for Gregory Peck.

CONNIE: *(looking to the heavens)* Catherine, if you're up there . . . or Greg . . . please guide Tate's ball to the centre of the fairway.

TATE swings.

Oops. I guess Catherine and Gregory are otherwise engaged.

TATE starts to cry.

MARGOT: Oh, Tate, don't cry. It wasn't that bad a shot.

CONNIE: Yeah, come on, Tater. We'll find it.

MARGOT: Of course we will.

TATE: No, it's not the shot . . . completely. I miss Catherine. I miss her terribly. I mean, this was where I saw Catherine most often. Out here on the golf course. It doesn't seem right being here without her. Dory, it's nothing against you. You're a very nice woman, and you dress impeccably. I just miss Catherine so much.

MARGOT: Oh, baby, that's okay. We all miss her.

MARGOT hugs TATE.

DORY: I understand how you feel, Tate. Cathy was an important part of your life. Without her, an essential piece of your existence is missing.

TATE: Why did she have to die? Why did God have to take *her*? Why couldn't He have taken someone else? Someone who wasn't as nice or as caring or as wholesome?

CONNIE: Why is she looking at me?

DORY: It's been said that God takes the good ones first so that he'll have someone to chum around with up there.

TATE: That's a nice thought.

MARGOT: It's a very nice thought. Do you feel better now?

TATE: A little bit.

MARGOT: Good.

TATE: Do you really think we'll find my ball?

MARGOT: Of course we will.

TATE: Really?

MARGOT: No, dear. There isn't a chance in heaven or hell.

MARGOT and TATE exit.

CONNIE: So that he'll have someone to chum around with up there?

DORY: Not bad, huh?

CONNIE: Where did you hear that? Hallmark?

DORY: I made it up.

CONNIE: Just now? On the spot?

DORY: It made her feel better, didn't it?

CONNIE: That's pretty crafty.

DORY: Just trying to help a friend.

DORY exits.

CONNIE: *(to herself)* I've got my eye on you, Doris.

CONNIE begins to exit.

These are definitely on backwards.

CONNIE exits.

THE SEVENTH TEE

They enter.

DORY: I'm sorry about that, Margot. That was a bad hole.

MARGOT: Hey, I wasn't much help.

CONNIE: So, that puts Tate and me up by two strokes. The universe is unfolding as it should.

MARGOT: Don't get too cocky. There's a long way to go yet.

CONNIE tees up her ball.

TATE: So, you grew up in Arizona, Dory?

DORY: Uh-huh.

TATE: So, you're an American?

DORY: That's right.

TATE: And you wound up in Arrowhead Lake.

DORY: Well, I fell in love with a Canadian.

TATE: Yeah, me too.

MARGOT: You live in Canada.

TATE: Well, that certainly increased my chances.

(to DORY) And what were the dreams you abandoned?

DORY: What do you mean?

TATE: You said you put your dreams on hold to follow your husband's dream. So what were your dreams?

DORY: Oh, nothing really. It was silly.

TATE: If it's a dream, it's not silly. No dream is silly.

DORY: It was nothing. I . . . I wanted to be a singer.

TATE: Really?

CONNIE hits her ball.

CONNIE: That'll play.

TATE tees up her ball.

TATE: A singer. Hmm. Well, it's too bad you never got to pursue it.

DORY: Oh, I pursued it. In fact, I *was* a singer before I got spirited away to Arrowhead Lake. Well, that didn't sound right, did it? It sounded like I didn't want to move up there.

MARGOT: Did you?

DORY: I was in love and completely open to any proposition that would strengthen and enhance our relationship.

MARGOT: So, you didn't want to move.

DORY: It was the right thing to do.

TATE: You were making your living as a singer?

DORY: Yep. I was singing in Las Vegas. That's where I met my husband. He was the sound man for the show I was in. And after about a ten-month courtship, we got married.

MARGOT: And how long after that did you get spirited away?

DORY: Not long.

TATE hits her ball.

CONNIE: You must have been awfully young when you were working in Vegas.

DORY: Twenty-two.

DORY tees up her ball.

TATE: And you were making your living as a singer at that age? You must have been good.

DORY: They said I had talent. They said I had a bright future. That I was going to set the music world on its ear.

MARGOT: And you gave it up for Arrowhead Lake?

DORY: It was the right thing to do.

DORY, with a grunt, takes an extra-furious swing at the golf ball.

CONNIE: Well, you beat the piss out of that one.

MARGOT: I don't think I've ever seen a golf ball split in two like that.

DORY: Who's up? Margot, you're up. Let's go. Let's go.

MARGOT: Yes, ma'am.

MARGOT tees up her ball.

TATE: So, it was your husband's dream to own a lodge in Canada?

DORY: Yep.

TATE: Way up there in the middle of nowhere?

DORY: Uh-huh.

TATE: And you gave up your dream of becoming a world-famous singer for that?

DORY: I sure did.

TATE: Wow. So, tell me this.

MARGOT: Tate.

TATE: What?

MARGOT: I'm about to hit.

TATE: Oh, sorry.

MARGOT hits her ball.

TATE: Good one.

(to DORY) So, tell me this.

MARGOT: Tate?

TATE: What?

MARGOT: It sounds to me like Dory doesn't want to discuss this matter any further.

TATE: Really?

DORY: No, it's fine.

TATE: She says it's fine. So, tell me this . . .

MARGOT: Tate. I don't think it's fine.

DORY: It's fine.

CONNIE: There's a mutilated golf ball out there that says it's not fine.

DORY: It's okay. Really. What is it, Tate? What else do you want to know about my idyllic life up there on Arrowhead Lake? Up there in the Canadian wilderness where men are men and women can smell them at fifty paces. Where I welcome our guests each summer with an inviting smile and six whiny children tugging on every free appendage like suckling piglets on a sow's teat. Where in the comforting heat of an August afternoon we swim in the calm waters of a secluded lake followed by fifteen terrifying minutes of ripping leeches off of our skin like they were stay-fast Band-Aids. And then there's the blackflies, big enough to carry off young children, although try as I might, I can't coax them into carrying mine off for an afternoon so that I can catch forty winks and a margarita. And then comes the winter. Ah, the Canadian winter, where I discover the pleasures of snowmobiling while wearing a flattering fleece-lined, Thermoflex-insulated suit that keeps me warm for a good five minutes before frostbite sets in, and I couldn't feel my ass even if George Clooney himself was straddling it. So, tell me. Tell me do, Tate. What enlightening nugget of information can I impart to you about my tranquil existence up there in God's country?

Beat.

TATE: What about sitting on the back porch watching all those stars?

DORY: Screw the stars!

They exit.

THE EIGHTH TEE

They enter. MARGOT *has a beer in her hand.*

TATE: Well, I don't see what's wrong with it.

CONNIE: I just think they give young girls the wrong idea.

TATE: How?

CONNIE: Because they tell them they're all going to be rescued by handsome princes, and the only thing they have to do is sit by a pond and look pretty.

MARGOT: What does a pond have to do with it?

CONNIE: Isn't that what princesses do? Sit by ponds and look at their reflections in the water while they're waiting for the handsome prince to ride in?

TATE: My daughters liked princesses when they were younger.

DORY: Mine too.

TATE: And they turned out fine. They're independent. They stand on their own two feet. Princesses are wonderful. They're fairy tales. And children need to get lost in fairy tales once in a while. It doesn't mean they have to emulate them when they grow up. But when they're young, what's so wrong with it?

CONNIE: But look at these women. They fall for the first guy who comes along; they dump their friends, and off they go to live in a castle where they're waited on hand and foot by a couple of bluebirds and a squirrel.

DORY: Sounds good to me.

TATE: Look, I grew up watching those classic princesses. Snow White, Cinderella, Sleeping Beauty. And they didn't have an adverse effect on me. I wouldn't expect a man to be my protector. To put a roof over my head and earn a living for us while I sit at home and raise the children with no thought for a career of my own. Oh my God, those princesses are bitches!

CONNIE: I just don't think they're good role models for young girls. That's my opinion.

DORY: Actually, Connie, in this matter, you don't get to have an opinion.

CONNIE: What?

DORY: It's true. You can't know what it's like to raise a child. No one knows unless they've had a child. It is an experience that is like no other, in both good and bad ways. You just can't understand.

CONNIE: All right, so I don't get an opinion. Fine. But Margot has a daughter. She gets an opinion. Margot, what do you think?

MARGOT: You're really going to ask me this question?

CONNIE: Why not? All right, so your daughter and you are estranged. That's old news. But you must remember what it was like when she was young.

MARGOT: I remember.

CONNIE: Well?

TATE: That's okay, Margot. Never mind.

(to CONNIE) How can you be so insensitive?

CONNIE: Insensitive how?

TATE: How? Really?

MARGOT: All right, who's up? Connie you're up. Let's play golf.

CONNIE tees up her ball.

CONNIE: Was I being insensitive, Margot?

MARGOT: Yes.

CONNIE: I was?

MARGOT: Yes.

CONNIE: Oh. I had no idea.

MARGOT: Of course you didn't. That's what insensitive means.

Beat.

CONNIE: Oh, right.

DORY: Tate, I'm sorry.

TATE: Sorry about what?

DORY: About my outburst on the last hole. You were just making conversation and I lashed out. I'm sorry.

TATE: It's already forgotten.

DORY: I appreciate that.

CONNIE hits her ball.

CONNIE: Oh, that's a dandy. Hold your applause.

TATE tees up her ball.

TATE: Belle was a good role model for young girls.

CONNIE: Who?

TATE: Belle from *Beauty and the Beast*. She wasn't superficial. She loved a man even though he was physically repulsive.

CONNIE: She didn't marry him until he turned into a handsome prince.

TATE: Okay, she was a bitch too.

TATE hits her ball. DORY tees up her ball.

DORY: All right, Margot, we're two strokes down. We've got to make a move right now. We just need one of us to put it out in the fairway somewhere and we're all set.

DORY hits her ball.

There we go. That'll do.

MARGOT sets her beer can down and tees up her ball.

Okay, Margot, let out some shaft. That sounds dirty, doesn't it? Let out some shaft. Well, it's not dirty. It means that you—

CONNIE: We know what it means, Doris.

TATE: I don't know what it means.

CONNIE: I'll explain it later.

TATE: And it's not dirty?

CONNIE: No.

TATE: Then I don't care.

MARGOT hits her ball. She picks up her tee and her beer and moves back to her bag.

DORY: Good shot, partner.

Just as they are about to exit, MARGOT speaks.

MARGOT: Stephanie and I used to watch those movies. Those princess movies. We used to watch them all the time. Well, she'd watch them. I would usually get home when the movie was half over, so I'd watch the second half with her. That's if I didn't fall asleep on the couch, of course. And on weekends we'd watch them in the morning . . . until I had to go to work. So, I'd get to see the first half of them then. I watched so many of those movies out of sequence that I'm not sure what happens in which one. So, I guess I don't have an opinion either. Because I don't know what my daughter thought of them or how they influenced her life or didn't influence it. I could ask her, but as you know, we don't speak.

MARGOT exits.

TATE: *(to CONNIE)* Why did you have to bring up her daughter? You know better than that.

TATE exits. CONNIE begins to exit but DORY stops her.

DORY: Connie, wait.

CONNIE: I think I should go and comfort my friend, Doris.

DORY: No, just wait for one second. What do you say you and me put a little money on this game?

CONNIE: What do you mean?

DORY: You and me. We won't tell the others. Your team against my team. Just to make it interesting.

CONNIE: How much?

DORY: What we originally decided on. Five hundred dollars.

CONNIE: You're two strokes down. You really think you can win?

DORY: Win? I just want to make it interesting.

CONNIE: Yeah, you keep saying that.

DORY: So?

Beat.

CONNIE: All right. You're on.

DORY: Good.

CONNIE: And it's just a bet between you and me.

DORY: Right.

CONNIE: Okay.

DORY: Good.

CONNIE: Can I go now?

DORY: Yes. Run. Off you go.

CONNIE exits.

All right. That's better.

DORY exits.

THE NINTH TEE

They enter. They will hit with irons on this hole.

CONNIE: How could you miss that putt, Tate?

TATE: You missed it too.

CONNIE: Yeah, but I went before you, so you should have gone to school on mine.

TATE: I don't know what that means.

CONNIE: It means we're only up by one stroke now.

TATE: So what? We're still winning.

MARGOT: Does anybody want to stop for a sandwich at the turn?

DORY takes out an iron and tees up her ball

DORY: Oh, no. I don't want to spoil my appetite for that big lunch I'm going to be treated to.

CONNIE: Hey, it's not over till the fat lady sings. And that would be Mrs. Mendelson in the foursome behind us.

TATE: Oh, guess who was at my yoga class yesterday? Rachel Borland.

MARGOT: Oh, I haven't seen her in a while.

TATE: *(to DORY)* Rachel used to be a member here, but then her and her husband joined the swankier club in town. They're social climbers. Always have to outdo everyone else. Anyway, it looked to me like Rachel has had some work done.

CONNIE: Really? What kind?

TATE: Well, it was hard to tell. I don't know if it's a face job that's pulled her boobs up or a boob job that's pulled her face down. Either way, she's been ironed and fluffed.

DORY hits her ball. MARGOT tees her ball up.

MARGOT: I'll bet that was her husband's idea.

CONNIE: Carl? Why do you think that?

MARGOT: Oh, he just strikes me as that kind. If Rachel didn't get some touching up he'd probably go out and find a newer model.

CONNIE: I don't know. I think we underestimate men sometimes. They're not all looking for the newer, younger version.

MARGOT: Maybe that's just what you *want* to believe.

CONNIE: I do believe it. I like men. I love men. And I couldn't love them if I thought they were all that shallow.

TATE: Well, a lot of them are.

MARGOT hits her ball.

CONNIE: Would you have work done if Bobby asked you to?

TATE: No. And Bobby would certainly know the surgeons who could do it properly. But I'm happy with the way I look.

DORY: Maybe you won't feel that way in ten years.

MARGOT: Or maybe Bobby won't.

CONNIE tees up her ball.

TATE: Well, call me an idiotic romantic, but I want to think that we'll grow old together, warts and all. Love should cut through all the superficial crap, right?

CONNIE: You're right.

TATE: Thank you.

CONNIE: You are an idiotic romantic.

CONNIE hits her ball.

MARGOT: What about you, Connie?

CONNIE: Me? Well, I'm in a different situation. I'm on television. My looks are part of my job qualifications whether I like it or not.

TATE: Really? You think you have to be attractive to do your job?

TATE tees up her ball.

CONNIE: Oh, Tate, don't be so naive. Of course I have to be attractive. They don't put trolls on television unless they're male. For some reason the viewing public accepts unattractive men on television, but they won't stand for a less-than-perfect female. It's not right, but I've accepted it.

MARGOT: So does that mean you'd have work done if it meant keeping your job?

CONNIE: No. If it means keeping my job, then they can go to hell. Besides, there are so many pretty and perky young newscasters out there right now that having work done wouldn't help me anyway. The dam's bursting, and there's a flood of leggy blonds crashing down on me.

TATE hits her ball.

TATE: Well, that sure sucked.

CONNIE: That sure did.

DORY: I'd have work done.

CONNIE: You?

DORY: Sure. Why not me?

CONNIE: Well, little country mouse and all. Why would you have work done?

DORY: I want to look good. I want to stay young. Who doesn't want that? Just because I'm living in the outback like some fur trapper doesn't mean I don't want to look good.

MARGOT: You really don't like it up there, do you?

DORY: No, I love it. With the stars and the breeze in the bloody trees. I adore it. Have you got another beer?

MARGOT takes a beer out of her bag and gives it to DORY.

CONNIE: So, that leaves you, Margot. What if your new beau asked you to have work done? Would you do it?

MARGOT: Well, first of all, Garrett would never ask that of me. He's not that type. And I don't plan on having any work done, ever. I don't want to look in the mirror one day and see someone I don't recognize staring back at me. That would be unsettling. No, I'm driving this jalopy all the way home as is.

CONNIE: Garrett who?

MARGOT: Garrett Ross.

CONNIE: I know Garrett Ross.

MARGOT: You do?

CONNIE: Sure, I interviewed him last year when he bought the Cooper Complex.

MARGOT: Oh. He didn't mention that he knew you. I told him I golf with you, and he didn't say anything.

CONNIE: Well, maybe he forgot. I mean, it was just a two-minute interview.

MARGOT: So you know him?

CONNIE: Yes. Very handsome.

MARGOT: He is, isn't he?

CONNIE: Very.

MARGOT: Well, that's my guy.

CONNIE: Good for you, Margot. Nice catch.

MARGOT: Thank you.

CONNIE: Yes, nice catch indeed.

MARGOT and DORY exit. TATE starts to exit. CONNIE stops her.

Tate?!

TATE: What?

CONNIE: I've slept with him.

TATE: Slept with who? Narrow it down for me.

CONNIE: Garrett Ross. Margot's new man. I've slept with him.

TATE: You have?

CONNIE: Yes.

TATE: You didn't tell me that.

CONNIE: Well, I don't tell you about every man I sleep with.

TATE: True. Who has that much time? So, when did this happen?

CONNIE: After the interview last year he asked me out to dinner, and one thing led to another, and, you know.

TATE: You had dinner and then you went back to his place for sex?

CONNIE: No. We did it in my dressing room after the interview.

TATE: What?!

CONNIE: Yes.

TATE: You said one thing led to another.

CONNIE: It did! It led to my dressing room!

TATE: Oh my God.

CONNIE: What am I going to do?

TATE: Nothing. You're not going to do anything.

CONNIE: But she's a friend. I've had sex with her man.

TATE: Well, the chances of that happening were pretty good anyway.

CONNIE: I've got to tell her, Tate. I can't live with this.

TATE: No! Now, you listen to me. This is the first man that Margot has been out with in years. And if this relationship goes sour then she might never try again. So, you are not going to blow this for her. Do you understand?

CONNIE: But she's going to—

TATE grabs CONNIE by the shoulders.

TATE: I said do you understand?!

Beat.

CONNIE: I understand. Not a word.

TATE: Good.

TATE lets go of CONNIE.

CONNIE: You got pretty aggressive there.

TATE: You like that?

CONNIE: Yeah. Bit of a turn-on, actually.

They exit. Lights down.

ACT TWO

THE TENTH TEE

CONNIE enters marking the scorecard. After a moment, TATE enters carrying her Thermos.

CONNIE: Where'd you go?

TATE: I topped up my smoothie. I've got a jug of it in a cooler in the car.

CONNIE: You've become quite the health nut, haven't you?

TATE: We only get one body. We've got to take care of it.

CONNIE: *(showing TATE the scorecard)* Look at this. They've tied us now. We had them by two strokes.

TATE: Dory's a good player. She's making some great shots.

CONNIE: Well, then we've got to start making better shots, don't we?

TATE: Oh, so we lose. So what? We're only playing for lunch.

CONNIE: Oh, you think so, huh?

TATE: Well, what else are we playing for?

Beat.

CONNIE: Pride. We're playing for pride too.

TATE: Pride? Connie, I've lost to you every time we've played for the past fourteen years. I have no pride out here. I'm used to losing.

CONNIE: You know what they call people who are used to losing?

TATE: I know what Bobby calls them. The Maple Leafs.

CONNIE: They're called losers. Now, let's get it together.

DORY and MARGOT enter laughing.

TATE: What's so funny?

DORY: There's a condom dispenser in the ladies' room. Why is there a condom dispenser in the ladies' room on a golf course? What happens out here anyway?

CONNIE: It's for members' night.

MARGOT: Members' night. Classy.

DORY: We have a dispenser in the washroom at the Arrowhead golf course too. For bear repellent. Oh God, I hate it up there.

MARGOT: Dory, you're away seeing as how we won that last hole.

DORY: All righty. Here we go.

DORY tees up her ball.

I'm so glad we're doing this. This is fun. Cathy said you were a fun group. And I really needed this.

TATE: I have a question.

MARGOT: What?

TATE: Why was Catherine up on that Ferris wheel all by herself? What grown-up person rides a Ferris wheel alone?

MARGOT: Maybe it was part of a school trip. Was she there with her class?

TATE: No. It was a Saturday. School trips don't happen on weekends.

DORY hits her ball.

MARGOT: Maybe she had some things on her mind and was up there thinking.

MARGOT tees up her ball.

CONNIE: No. Catherine wasn't that type.

DORY: Wasn't what type?

CONNIE: A deep thinker. She had life figured out. She didn't have a care in the world.

TATE: Maybe she was lonely. I mean, she had no boyfriend. No love in her life. Maybe she was down about that.

CONNIE: And why would that put her on a Ferris wheel by herself?

TATE: Depressed people do unpredictable things.

CONNIE: Catherine wasn't depressed. She was a rock. A very strong woman.

MARGOT hits her ball.

CONNIE: I think she went up there to take photographs. She was into photography, right? What better place to get some panoramic photographs?

CONNIE tees up her ball.

TATE: Maybe.

CONNIE: I'm sure of it. Catherine was anything but unpredictable. In fact, you could set your watch by her.

CONNIE hits her ball.

Oooh, right beside you, Doris.

TATE tees up her ball.

DORY: I disagree. I think Cathy *was* a deep thinker. When she visited the lodge we talked about everything from politics to religion to philosophy.

CONNIE: Philosophy?

DORY: Yeah. I mean, I don't know a whole lot about it, but Cathy did. I found her to be a very deep thinker. She was a teacher, after all.

MARGOT: She never talked to us about those things.

DORY: Maybe because you wouldn't let her.

CONNIE: What's that supposed to mean?

TATE hits her ball.

DORY: Well, you called her a rock. Didn't have a care in the world. Maybe she felt like she had to be that person and not who she really was.

MARGOT: We knew her for over fifteen years. How could we not know the real person after fifteen years?

DORY: People are full of surprises. Or maybe she just felt that you three outshone her, so she hid her light under a bushel.

MARGOT: Outshone her?

DORY: Sure. You with your own construction company. Connie, a popular television personality, and . . . you, Tate.

TATE: Me, Tate? What, I don't have a quality that shines?

DORY: You do. In fact, I think Cathy was intimidated by you most of all. Because you're so pretty.

TATE: Pretty? That's it? My looks? And thank you, by the way, because it's something I really work on. Sometimes those three teenagers of mine just suck the damn life right out of me. Every wrinkle you see here has got their fingerprints on it. Ungrateful little hedgehogs!

DORY: The thing is, maybe Cathy felt that her intellect wasn't as alluring as what you three had to offer, and so she hid it. I mean, we all knew that kid in school who was really brainy but tried not to show it for fear of being an outcast.

MARGOT: We're all grown up now, Dory. I doubt if that example applies to women our age.

TATE: Or my age.

CONNIE: Doris, you didn't know her as well as we did. I think Catherine was very secure in her own skin. She wasn't envious of my fame or Margot's success or Tate's looks.

MARGOT: I agree.

TATE: And I'll think it over.

DORY: Well, maybe you're right.

CONNIE: I know I'm right.

DORY: Good. Let's play on then.

DORY exits.

MARGOT: Do you think she's right? Do you think we held Catherine down?

CONNIE: What, and made her hide her light under a bushel? No. We were her friends. She could be whoever she wanted around us.

Pause. No one responds.

Well, couldn't she?

MARGOT: I guess.

CONNIE: Of course she could. It's ridiculous to think that she was intimidated by my fame.

MARGOT: Right. Or my success.

They look at TATE.

Beat.

TATE: Absolutely.

TATE exits. MARGOT and CONNIE follow.

THE ELEVENTH TEE

They enter.

MARGOT: It all happened quite innocently, actually. We were on site looking at blueprints of this job we were doing for him, and he was standing beside me, and we were almost touching, and I could just feel the energy between us. It was palpable. And I guess he felt it too because he asked me out right there. So we went to dinner that night and one thing led to another. You know how it is.

TATE: No, we don't know!

MARGOT: What?

TATE: We have no idea how one thing leads to another, do we, Connie?

CONNIE: No.

MARGOT: Oh, please. Connie, you of all people would know that. I still can't believe Garrett didn't remember you.

CONNIE: I can't believe it either.

TATE: All right, enough talk about Garrett. My God, so you found a man. Get over yourself already. Connie what's the score? Who's up?

CONNIE: We're still tied. Doris is up.

DORY: All right.

DORY tees up her ball.

So, Margot, what did your ex-husband do?

MARGOT: He's the hotel manager at the Four Seasons.

DORY: Oh. He's in the hospitality industry like me. Except he's in a fancy big-city hotel, and I'm serving breakfast to Hawkeye and Chingachgook.

She takes an angry swing at the ball. MARGOT tees up her ball.

MARGOT: Garrett says he almost bought that hotel last year. That would have been awkward. My ex-husband working for my current boyfriend. What could be more awkward than that?

TATE: I can't think of a thing.

MARGOT hits her ball.

DORY: I guess I should be thankful that we have indoor plumbing at least, or I'd be down by the river beating my kids on the rocks to get them clean.

MARGOT: Don't you mean your clothes?

Beat.

DORY: Yeah.

CONNIE tees up her ball.

CONNIE: Do we still call them boyfriends at our age?

MARGOT: What?

CONNIE: Men. At our age, do we still refer to them as "boyfriends"?

MARGOT: Well, what else would we call them?

CONNIE: I don't know. "Partners"?

MARGOT: No. "Partners" is further along in the relationship. Partners cohabitate. Besides, "partners" sounds like you're in business together. It sounds cold.

TATE: How about "fella"? Like, this is my fella.

CONNIE: That's fine if you're Bette Davis.

TATE: Too old-fashioned?

CONNIE: Yes.

CONNIE hits her ball. TATE tees up her ball.

TATE: Good shot, Connie.

MARGOT: Dory, what would you call a boyfriend?

DORY: "My ticket out of there."

TATE: What about "lover"?

MARGOT: Oh, no. "Lover" is too familiar. I had a woman introduce me to a man once, and she said, "This is my lover," and immediately I started to picture them doing it. No, "lover" is a name you call the person in private as a term of endearment. Or it's something you say to them in the throes of passion. And you don't want to introduce someone by a name that conjures up visions of lovemaking.

CONNIE: True. I'd like you to meet "Oh my God!"

MARGOT: Have you met "Oh baby, you're good!"

TATE: Allow me to introduce "Not yet! Not yet!"

DORY: Please say hello to "You're on my hair!"

CONNIE: Ladies, I'd like you to meet "Well, that was two scoops of good lovin'."

TATE hits her ball.

MARGOT: Oh my God.

CONNIE: I already said that one.

MARGOT: Oh my God.

CONNIE: What's wrong?

MARGOT: You slept with him.

CONNIE: What? Slept with who?

MARGOT: Garrett. You slept with Garrett.

CONNIE: With Garrett? Why would you say that?

MARGOT: "That was two scoops of good lovin'." That's what he said to me the first time we made love.

DORY: He actually said that to you? Wow.

MARGOT: You did, didn't you?

CONNIE: Oh, come on.

MARGOT: You did.

TATE: Margot, I think you're jumping to conclusions.

MARGOT: Really, Tate? And how many other men do you think would say that?

TATE: Damn it, Connie!

CONNIE: Well, I didn't know it was Garrett who said it. I just remembered I heard it from somebody.

DORY: He said that to both of you? Wow.

MARGOT: You slept with my boyfriend?

TATE: Now, we haven't decided what to call him yet, remember?

MARGOT: How could you do that, Connie?

CONNIE: I didn't know you were going to start dating him. This happened a year ago. And it only happened once, I swear.

MARGOT: Oh my God.

(to TATE) Did you know about this?

TATE: I just found out.

MARGOT: And you kept it from me?

TATE: It was two holes ago!

MARGOT: So my best friend slept with my boyfriend. Well, that's just great. How humiliating.

(to DORY) I suppose you heard about it too.

DORY: How in the hell would I hear about it up on Walton's Mountain?

TATE: Connie's your best friend?

MARGOT: What?

TATE: You just said Connie was your best friend.

MARGOT: So?

TATE: I thought I was your best friend. I've known you the longest. I've known you for twenty years. You're godmother to one of my children.

MARGOT: So what? So was Catherine. So's Connie.

CONNIE: Yeah, right. To Nigel.

TATE: There is nothing wrong with Nigel.

DORY: That's the one with the lazy eye, right?

CONNIE: Right.

TATE: Do you mind?!

(to MARGOT) I just thought that you and I had something special. A deeper friendship.

CONNIE: Now, wait a minute. Why would you have a deeper friendship with Margot than with me?

TATE: Because you're harder to get close to. You keep your distance.

MARGOT: Unless there's a boyfriend involved.

CONNIE: Now, that's not fair. I didn't know he was going to wind up being your boyfriend. How did I know he'd be attracted to you?

MARGOT: Are you saying a man like that couldn't be attracted to me?

CONNIE: I didn't say that at all.

MARGOT storms off.

(to TATE) Did I say that? I didn't say that.

TATE: There is nothing wrong with Nigel!

TATE storms off.

DORY: You actually kind of did say that.

CONNIE: I didn't ask you, Doris.

DORY: Why can't you call me "Dory"?

CONNIE: What?

DORY: You call me "Doris," "Dottie," "Gidget." Everything but "Dory." Why? Do you think if you call me "Dory" that would mean you're accepting me into your little circle of friends?

CONNIE: Yes. And I've got enough friends.

CONNIE exits.

DORY: I think you've got two less than you did five minutes ago!

DORY exits.

THE TWELFTH TEE

They all enter a few strides apart. CONNIE tees up her ball and hits. She picks up her tee. TATE tees up her ball and hits. She picks up her tee. DORY tees up her ball and hits. She picks up her tee. MARGOT tees up her ball and hits. She picks up her tee. They exit.

THE THIRTEENTH TEE

They all enter a few strides apart. DORY tees up her ball and hits. She picks up her tee. MARGOT tees up her ball and hits. She picks up her tee. CONNIE tees up her ball.

DORY: Aw, come on, girls, we can't play the rest of the round like this. We're playing for Cathy. She wouldn't like this one bit. She'd be very disappointed.

CONNIE hits her ball. She picks up her tee.

Nice shot. Really, come on. You girls have been friends forever, and I think it would be foolish to throw that away just because Connie can't keep it in her pants.

The other three look at DORY.

You know what I mean.

TATE tees up her ball.

Tate, you seem like the sensible one of the group—which isn't saying much—so put a stop to this now before it goes too far.

TATE hits her ball and picks up her tee.

Aw, come on, you three. This is ridiculous.

CONNIE: Margot, I'm sorry.

DORY: That's better.

CONNIE: Shut up, Doris.

(to MARGOT) I'm sorry that I slept with Garrett. If I had it to do all over again, I wouldn't, of course. I know I've slept with a lot of men. Some would say too many.

TATE raises her hand.

I'm not taking a poll.

TATE lowers her hand.

The problem is, I had the love of my life, and I lost him. Vic was it for me. I knew we'd be together for the rest of our lives. We'd have a family . . . a home . . . a life that those princesses always wind up with. It was going to be that perfect. I just knew it. I should have said let's go home and get that life started right away, today, but we were still young and doing what we thought was important work as journalists. Covering a war. Being in the centre of the action. We'd only been married for a year. There was plenty of time for the family and the home. But at that moment, being on the front line as journalists was what mattered most. I didn't see the woman. She came out of a house behind me as I was doing a report. It was Vic who saw her and stopped filming and went to her. He didn't know she was a bomber because the device was under her coat. He just wanted her out of the shot. And that was how I lost the love of my life. To a stranger, on a dirty street, six thousand miles from home. It's a sad story, right? Oh, yeah, it's a doozy. But sad stories come out of a war every day, and I didn't wallow in self-pity. At least not outwardly. No, my way of doing it was to have brief liaisons with men. Nothing with any depth. Some talk, some sex, and we move on. You see, I know I'm never going to find another love of my life. That's impossible. The love of your life is just that. The love of your life. Singular. So, now I just try and find moments with men, because I love them too much to be without them, and I loved one too much to stay with any of them. And I'll probably keep doing it—no, I *will* keep doing it—but I'll make sure I stay away from your men from now on. Doris, what's your husband's name?

DORY: Richard.

CONNIE: I'd better jot that down.

(to MARGOT) So, are we good now?

MARGOT: I just wish you hadn't slept with Garrett. Geez, Connie!

CONNIE: Well, I wish I hadn't slept with him either.

MARGOT: Why? Was he no good?

CONNIE: No, I mean because he's your guy.

MARGOT: Oh.

CONNIE: That's why.

MARGOT: Fine.

CONNIE: No, he was great.

MARGOT: He was?

CONNIE: What?

MARGOT: You said he was great.

CONNIE: So?

MARGOT: So, he was good with you? He pleasured you?

CONNIE: What's the right answer here, Margot? He was good or he was bad? What do you want to hear?

DORY: Oh, that's enough. Stop it. You can't stand here and compare your lovemaking sessions with Garrett. That's vulgar. Tate and I don't want to hear that.

TATE: Speak for yourself.

MARGOT: Well, I'm sorry too.

CONNIE: What are you sorry about?

MARGOT: I don't know. I just didn't want you to be the only one looking like an idiot.

CONNIE: You're a good friend.

MARGOT: And so are you.

TATE: Yeah. Her best friend.

MARGOT: Oh, Tate. I didn't mean that. Of course I like you better than Connie.

TATE: Really?

CONNIE: Really?

MARGOT: Of course.

TATE: I knew it.

CONNIE: Why do you like her better?

MARGOT: Well, let's see now. Show of hands. Which one of you slept with my boyfriend?

CONNIE raises her hand.

Oh! There you go.

MARGOT exits followed by TATE.

DORY: I'm sorry about your husband, Connie. Cathy didn't tell me about that.

CONNIE: It happened a long time ago. Long before she met you.

DORY turns to leave and then stops.

DORY: So, Garrett. Was he good or was he bad? I know. Shut up, Doris.

DORY exits. After a moment's thought, CONNIE says to herself:

CONNIE: He was gooood.

CONNIE exits.

THE FOURTEENTH TEE

They enter. They will all hit irons on this tee.

MARGOT: I believe that puts us up by one stroke, Dory. Are you ready to suffer your first-ever defeat, Connie?

DORY: You're really getting into this, Margot.

MARGOT: Well, I have a new-found incentive to win.

DORY tees up her ball.

CONNIE: We're not beaten yet, ladies. Right, Tate?

TATE: I don't care. It's only lunch.

CONNIE: I wish you'd stop saying that.

DORY hits her ball.

MARGOT: Yes!

MARGOT tees up her ball.

CONNIE: So, I was wondering, Doris . . .

TATE: Bobby Kennedy!

The others turn and look at TATE. TATE holds up her hand, encouraging CONNIE to give her a high-five.

Up top.

CONNIE turns back to DORY.

CONNIE: I was wondering. How much did Catherine tell you about us? I mean, you seem to know about certain aspects of our lives, and yet you're unaware of others.

DORY: Well, we didn't talk about you constantly. Just occasionally.

MARGOT hits her ball.

MARGOT: And that's the problem, Dory. Connie would rather you talked about her constantly.

CONNIE tees up her ball.

CONNIE: No, that's not it at all. I just find it disconcerting to be around someone who appears to know certain things about me, and yet I know nothing about her.

CONNIE hits her ball. TATE *tees up her ball.*

MARGOT: So, do you know our deepest, darkest secrets, Dory? Is that what Catherine told you about?

DORY: No. There are no secrets.

CONNIE: No?

DORY: No. Hardly any.

MARGOT: *Hardly* any?

DORY: Hardly any at all.

MARGOT: But that means there are some.

DORY: Is that what it means?

MARGOT: Yes. Hardly any means some.

DORY: Well, Cathy did mention a couple of things.

CONNIE: Like what?

DORY: No, I'd feel uneasy telling you.

CONNIE: Oh, come on. We won't get upset. We'll probably find these things amusing.

(to TATE and MARGOT) Right?

TATE: Sure.

MARGOT: Absolutely.

DORY: Well . . . she said that one of you is a man-chaser.

MARGOT: Well, that's no secret.

CONNIE: No, that's a matter of public record.

MARGOT: It is?

CONNIE: I took out an ad once with my phone number and photo.

MARGOT: Internet?

CONNIE: Billboard. But it wasn't on a main thoroughfare.

TATE hits.

TATE: That was bad.

CONNIE: No, don't look at it as bad. Look at it as consistent.

MARGOT: So, what was the other one?

DORY: The other what?

MARGOT: You said there were a couple of things that Catherine mentioned. What was the other one?

DORY: It's not important.

CONNIE: It is now that you said it isn't.

MARGOT: What is it?

DORY: I shouldn't even have said anything. These things were told to me by Cathy in confidence. I don't want to betray that trust.

MARGOT: It's not legally binding, Dory. Now, what is it?

TATE: Yeah, come on. You've got my interest now too.

DORY: Well, she said that one of you is a problem drinker.

CONNIE: Again, no secret.

MARGOT: Wait. I'm not a problem drinker. I never drink at work. I just have a couple to wind down.

CONNIE: How many have you had this morning?

MARGOT: I'm not working this morning. I'm socializing. And I take exception to being called a problem drinker. I drink with little or no problem at all.

DORY: Actually, Margot, it wasn't you.

MARGOT: What?

DORY: Cathy wasn't talking about you.

MARGOT: *(to CONNIE)* You see? It wasn't me. Wait a minute. Who drinks more than me?

DORY looks at TATE.

CONNIE: Tate?

TATE: What?!

MARGOT: No!

CONNIE: Sweet, innocent only-gets-laid-once-a-week Tate?

MARGOT: No. There's no way Tate drinks more than me. No way.

CONNIE: Actually, Margot, this might be a contest you don't want to win.

MARGOT: Is this true, Tate?

TATE: No, of course not. When have you ever seen me drink too much? Have you ever seen me drunk?

MARGOT: She's right. I've never seen that.

CONNIE: Me neither.

TATE: It's ridiculous.

DORY: That's because you hide it well.

TATE: I don't hide anything. There's nothing to hide.

DORY: What's in your Thermos?

TATE: What?

DORY: Your water bottle. What's in it?

TATE: My smoothie. I always bring a smoothie when we golf.

MARGOT: That's true. She does.

DORY: Have you ever tasted it?

MARGOT: Why would I do that?

CONNIE: Let me try it, Tate.

TATE: It's my smoothie. There's no need to try it.

CONNIE: One sip.

TATE: No. I don't know where that mouth of yours has been.

TATE puts the bottle in her golf bag.

CONNIE: Very funny. Let's have it.

TATE: Connie . . .

CONNIE *takes the bottle out of* TATE's *golf bag.*

CONNIE: One sip. That's all I want. Let's prove the country mouse wrong, huh? She thinks she's such a know-it-all.

CONNIE *takes a drink.*

She wasn't lying. It's a smoothie. A White Russian smoothie.

MARGOT: Well, I'll be damned. How long has this been going on?

TATE: How long has what being going on? You make it sound nefarious.

CONNIE: It is nefarious. First of all, you hide your pitiful sex life from us and now this.

TATE: My sex life is not pitiful. Oh, dammit, it is pitiful!

MARGOT: What is it, Tate? Why are you drinking like this?

TATE: Like what?

MARGOT: Like more than me. What's wrong?

TATE: What do you think? You said it yourself.

MARGOT: Said what?

TATE: "You've got a good man and beautiful children."

MARGOT: What?

TATE: When I said I had frittered away my life, you said, "You've got a good man and beautiful children."

MARGOT: So? You do.

TATE: And that's how my life is measured. I'm a good wife and a good mother.

DORY: What's wrong with that?

TATE: I want more now. When my kids were younger they demanded all of my attention, and I was happy about that being my job. Being a mother. I was proud of that job. But now they've got their own lives. They're always out with friends. They don't need me as much. And I find myself alone more. And thinking more.

CONNIE: And drinking more?

MARGOT: Do you feel inadequate? Is that it?

TATE: I don't know. Maybe.

MARGOT: So, what do you want to do?

TATE: What do you mean?

MARGOT: You said you want more. Like what? A job? A career? Do you have a dream you want to chase?

TATE: Well, sure I have a dream, but it's silly.

MARGOT: No, it's not.

TATE: How do you know? You don't even know what it is.

MARGOT: If it's a dream, it's not silly. No dream is silly. So, what is it?

Beat.

TATE: I'd love to own my own café.

MARGOT: You what?

TATE: Just a little restaurant, you know. Where I would be the boss, and I would choose the decor and the menu and the music that plays in the background. And it would be a nice little place for people to go and relax and talk. And I would make all the desserts. Desserts that people would savour and compliment me on. And I would circulate. I would swan around and talk to people. I would enjoy the company of grown-ups for an afternoon. I think I'd be good at that.

MARGOT: I think you would too.

CONNIE: So, do it. Tell little Bobby to get off his tricycle and buy a place for you.

TATE: No. That would be too easy. It wouldn't make it my own.

MARGOT: Go to the bank and get a loan.

TATE: Based on what? Based on how good a mom I've been for the past sixteen years? They'll want proof that they're backing a viable venture run by someone who's going to be able to pay them back.

CONNIE: You're right about that.

TATE: See? Silly. So, I have a drink to take the edge off. That's all it is.

MARGOT: Well, that's not good, Tate.

TATE: Oh, it's fine.

MARGOT: No, it's not fine. Not if you're hiding it.

TATE: So, I won't hide it anymore. I'll be like you and openly drink to excess. Now, let's get back to playing golf or we'll be here all day.

TATE exits.

CONNIE: *(to MARGOT)* You're not setting a very good example for our little girl. All that drinking. All that shtupping.

DORY: I shouldn't have said anything.

MARGOT: No, I'm glad you did. If nothing else we'll keep an eye on her now. But I wonder how Catherine knew about this and we didn't.

DORY: I told you. Cathy was very astute.

MARGOT and DORY exit. CONNIE takes a drink.

CONNIE: This is really good.

CONNIE exits.

THE FIFTEENTH TEE

They enter.

MARGOT: *(to TATE)* What about the music?

TATE: Well, I don't think I would play much instrumental music. No, I would play songs with great singers, like Ella and Luther Vandross and some new singers too. It wouldn't be entirely background music. It would be music that every once in a while would prick up somebody's ears.

MARGOT: Sounds like you've given this café a lot of thought.

TATE: I have. Pretty dumb, huh?

MARGOT: No, it's not dumb at all. What would you call it?

TATE: Well, I've given that a lot of thought too. I'd call it Tête-à-Tate.

CONNIE *swings, and her swing is very bad.*

CONNIE: Oh, geez, Tate. Look what you did.

TATE: Me?

CONNIE: Tête-à-Tate?

TATE: I think it's a great name. Tête-à-tête means a conversation, and the café would be a place where people could go and talk with friends.

TATE *tees up her ball.*

MARGOT: I think it's a great name too. And I like the music idea. Real songs instead of elevator music.

DORY: I wonder why nobody sang Cathy's favourite song at the funeral.

CONNIE: Why would you want someone to sing "I Feel Good" at a funeral?

DORY: "I Feel Good" wasn't her favourite song.

CONNIE: Sure it was. She loved James Brown.

DORY: Well, I know she did, but that wasn't her favourite song. Her favourite song was "The Water Is Wide."

TATE: The English folk song?

DORY: Right.

DORY sings the first line.

"The water is wide. I can't cross o'er."

MARGOT: I love that song.

TATE hits her ball.

DORY: So, why wasn't it sung at her funeral?

CONNIE: Because apparently you're the only one who knew it was her favourite song.

DORY tees up her ball.

DORY: Well, that's pretty sad. And I only saw her two weeks out of the year.

MARGOT: That is pretty sad.

CONNIE: Now, wait a minute. How do we know that was her favourite song? Just because Doris says it was doesn't make it so.

DORY: She used to ask me to sing it whenever she came up to Arrowhead. And she'd sing along with me. That's one of the special memories I have of Cathy.

TATE: I didn't know Catherine could sing.

DORY: She couldn't. She had an awful voice. I think that makes the memory even more special. She would just sing out like it didn't matter to her what she sounded like. She would just let go.

DORY hits her ball.

MARGOT: My favourite memory of Catherine is her coming to my house two Christmases ago, just after my daughter and I had the falling out. She knew I was alone and she marched into my house on Christmas morning with a turkey in one hand and a bottle of Jack Daniel's in the other. She was determined to give me a Christmas, and she wouldn't take no for an answer. We never did get around to cooking that turkey.

MARGOT tees up her ball.

TATE: She asked me to do her makeup for her once. On my wedding day. She was one of my bridesmaids.

MARGOT: *(to DORY)* Along with Connie and me.

DORY: Which one was the maid of honour?

CONNIE: None of us.

TATE: A girl named Paula Torello was the maid of honour. Paula and I went all through school together.

MARGOT: Worst maid of honour in history.

TATE: Paula was going through a breakup with her boyfriend at the time and she hated men.

MARGOT: She kept telling Tate that she was making a big mistake getting married.

TATE: When I was walking down the aisle she yelled, "Go back!" Anyway, Catherine knew how nervous I was, and she got me to do her makeup for her hoping it would take my mind off of everything. We talked about marriage, and she told me how wonderful it was going to be and how happy I was going to be, and she really got me through the day. That's my best memory of her.

MARGOT hits her ball.

DORY: And what about you, Connie? What's your best memory of Cathy?

CONNIE: When I lost Vic she sent me a letter that just said, "We love you. Come home." I've still got that letter.

DORY: It sounds like Cathy was really there for you when you needed her. For all of you.

MARGOT: She was. I think out of the four of us, Catherine had the biggest heart.

CONNIE: Really? What about me?

MARGOT: Out of the four of us, you would come ninth.

DORY: And I'm assuming you three were there for her as well.

TATE: Well, sure we were. Whenever she needed us.

DORY: That's good.

TATE: Although Catherine didn't seem to need us all that often.

MARGOT: That's right. She was very steady. She had it together.

CONNIE: Except for the relationship aspect of her life. She never did master that. I offered to introduce her to some men.

DORY: And what did she say?

MARGOT: "Leftovers again?"

CONNIE: No, now these were very nice gentlemen. I think she would have enjoyed their company.

MARGOT: Maybe her problem was that you had already enjoyed their company.

CONNIE: Oh geez, Margot, can we move on from this whole Garrett thing? I had sex with your man in my dressing room. I'm sorry, okay?

MARGOT: In your dressing room?

CONNIE: Yes.

(to TATE) I didn't tell her that?

TATE: No.

MARGOT: Is there a bed in your dressing room?

CONNIE: No, there's not.

MARGOT: So where did you do it?

CONNIE: Here and there. It was a movable feast. I really think we should stop discussing this.

TATE: So do I.

CONNIE: You see?

TATE: It's making me jealous.

TATE exits. CONNIE exits.

DORY: Cathy really loved you three.

MARGOT: What?

DORY: Cathy. She loved you three women.

MARGOT: I know. And we loved her.

DORY: I know you did. But you didn't know much about her.

DORY exits. MARGOT exits.

THE SIXTEENTH TEE

TATE: No, it's like in Australia nobody really says "throw another shrimp on the barbie," and in England nobody really says "chee-rio, old bean."

DORY: So nobody in Canada really says "eh"?

TATE: No. You never noticed that? How long have you lived here?

DORY: Sixteen years. My peak years. My prime.

CONNIE marks the scorecard.

CONNIE: Okay, thanks to a miraculous putt by my partner *(CONNIE and TATE high-five.)* we are now up by two.

TATE: I can taste that free lunch already.

CONNIE tees up her ball.

MARGOT: Are you okay, Dory?

DORY: Oh, fine. Yeah. Couldn't be better. I was just thinking that this time tomorrow I'll be on my way home.

TATE: Back to your children. What are their names?

DORY: Donna, Rosemary, Lucas, and three others. Listen, do you guys think everything in this life happens for a reason?

TATE: I do. I think there's a master plan.

DORY: Really?

TATE: Definitely.

DORY: So you think that no matter what we do, we can't change our destiny?

TATE: No, I didn't mean that. I just think there are no coincidences. If something happens to us—an occurrence—there's a reason for it.

CONNIE: Because you'll find a reason for it, no matter what. No, I think everything in this life is random. There's no rhyme or reason to any of it.

CONNIE hits her ball.

MARGOT: What do you think, Dory?

DORY: I don't know. That's what I'm trying to figure out.

TATE tees up her ball.

Sixteen years ago I was singing in Las Vegas. Loving my life. Thinking about my future in music. And then things conspired to move me to Arrowhead Lake, and I lost myself. I lost who I was.

TATE hits her ball.

So, why? Why did that happen? If there's a reason for everything, what was the reason for that?

CONNIE: Maybe it was your God. Maybe he did it.

DORY tees up her ball.

MARGOT: No. You said it yourself earlier, Dory. You fell in love with a Canadian. That's the reason for it.

DORY: Right. And then I got married too soon, and I gambled away our life savings, and off we went. Well, that explains everything then. Wonderful.

DORY hits her ball.

MARGOT: You gambled away your life savings?

DORY: Yes.

MARGOT: Really? What were you betting on?

DORY: Anything. And everything. That's why we moved to Arrowhead Lake. I lost ninety-five thousand dollars in the first three months after we got married. Richard wanted to get me away from that life. From the temptation. And I felt guilty, so I agreed to the move.

MARGOT: And now?

MARGOT tees up her ball.

DORY: Now, I wish I'd stayed. But that's not the question. The question is why did all of that happen? What is this leading me to?

TATE: Maybe it's not about you.

DORY: What do you mean?

TATE: Maybe it's about someone else. Maybe it's about your husband, or your children, or your grandchildren. Maybe everything that has happened to you is happening because it's part of the plan for someone else. And maybe something that happened to someone in your life many years ago—maybe even before you were born—happened because it was part of the plan for you.

MARGOT: Wow, Tate, that's pretty deep.

CONNIE: It sure is. Do you need to sit down? Catch your breath?

TATE: It's true. This is what I mean by no coincidences.

MARGOT hits her ball.

DORY: Well, I don't think I like that idea. That means we have no control over our outcomes.

CONNIE: I agree with Maverick here. I'd like to think I have some say in how my life is lived.

TATE: You do have a say. But the hurdles you have to jump are put there because of the plan.

CONNIE: How can you be so lucid after a jug of White Russians?

DORY: We haven't heard your opinion yet, Margot.

MARGOT: My opinion is very simple. We're born, we walk through life's minefield until we step on one, and we die. And somewhere along the way we taste little victories and little defeats. And if we're lucky we love someone and have someone love us back. That love might be for a day, or it might be for a lifetime. But as long as we've felt it, we're better for it. And we should never take it for granted.

MARGOT exits.

CONNIE: That's not bad.

TATE: *(to DORY)* A gambling addict, huh? Good thing we didn't agree to that five-hundred-dollar bet.

TATE exits. DORY starts to exit.

CONNIE: Dory.

DORY: Are you talking to me?

CONNIE: Is there anyone else here named Dory? Yes, I'm talking to you. I'm sorry about your gambling problem.

DORY: Thank you.

CONNIE: So, the bet's off.

DORY: What? No. I made the bet, and I'm going to stick to it. If there was one thing I learned during my fall from grace, it was that you never welsh on a bet.

CONNIE: No, look, the bet's off. Please. Do it for me.

DORY: For you?

CONNIE: Yes. You're going to lose. Do you want me to feel badly because I took money from a gambling addict who mistakenly thought she had the stuff to beat me at golf? No, I feel badly enough for having had sex with Margot's man.

DORY: Well, that wasn't your fault. And it only happened once.

Beat.

CONNIE: Right.

DORY: You mean it happened more than once?

CONNIE: Three times. But it was condensed into a five-hour period. It wasn't spread out over a week or anything.

DORY: Does that make it better?

CONNIE: Yes. It makes it mean less, doesn't it?

DORY: Oh, and is that your objective? To make your sexual encounters mean as little as possible?

CONNIE: Now you're catching on. And not a word to Margot.

DORY: My lips are sealed. Unlike yours apparently.

CONNIE: So, the bet is off.

DORY: Fine. But I'm doing it for you. Not for me.

CONNIE: Thank you.

DORY: Does this mean you've accepted me into your circle of friends?

CONNIE: What?

DORY: You called me Dory. So, am I your friend now?

CONNIE: Oh, for God's sake, don't be so needy. And the lunch bet is still on.

DORY: What?

CONNIE: You heard me.

DORY: Why is the lunch bet still on?

CONNIE: Because it is.

They start to exit.

DORY: I'm an addict. You're taking advantage of my illness.

CONNIE: That's not an illness. Dysentery is an illness. You ever had that? Gambling. Gambling doesn't put you on a toilet for three days.

They exit.

THE SEVENTEENTH TEE

TATE and DORY enter. The group will hit with irons on this tee.

DORY: Last year our youngest boy fell off of his bike and landed right on his chin.

TATE: Oh, no.

DORY: Yeah. Tore a big chunk out of it. It was awful. It took fifteen stitches to close it. He's got a big, ugly scar there now that he'll have for the rest of his life. Poor kid.

Beat.

TATE: You're just trying to make me feel better, aren't you?

DORY doesn't answer.

Dory?

DORY: Yeah.

TATE: He didn't fall off his bike at all, did he?

DORY: No.

TATE: There were no stitches. No scar.

DORY: No. I'm sorry.

TATE: He's probably a very handsome little boy.

DORY: He's adorable.

TATE: Well thank you. That you would falsely disfigure your child for my sake means a lot to me. *(looking off)* What are they doing back there? Probably discussing Garrett again. I hope Connie's not bragging. You might have noticed she's a little narcissistic. Did Catherine actually say she was intimidated by my looks?

DORY: She alluded to it.

TATE: Wow. That makes me feel . . . I don't know.

DORY: Good?

TATE: Pretty good, yeah.

MARGOT and CONNIE enter. DORY tees up her ball.

MARGOT: So now we're up by one stroke. What a remarkable turnaround. And with only two holes left to play.

TATE: Sorry about that, Connie.

CONNIE: Don't worry about it. I should have told you there was a penalty for picking up your ball and throwing it onto the green from behind a cluster of birch trees. Besides, you've only been playing for fourteen years. I can't expect you to know the rules.

DORY hits her ball.

MARGOT: Oooh, partner. Very nice shot. You're on.

MARGOT tees up her ball.

TATE: It's a stupid rule anyway.

CONNIE: What, that you can't pick up your ball and throw it? It is stupid. It's like they expect us to bring a bunch of sticks out here and hit the ball with those. Ridiculous.

MARGOT: All right, let's see what we can do here.

MARGOT hits her ball.

DORY: Oooh, very nice. That's even closer than mine.

CONNIE tees up her ball.

TATE: So, what are you going to do, Dory? About your situation up on Arrowhead Lake.

DORY: Nothing.

TATE: Nothing? Really?

DORY: What can I do? My family is happy up there. My kids, my husband. They love it. And I love them, so the best thing to do is to stick with it. Truth be told, it's too late for me anyway, as far as the music business goes.

CONNIE hits her ball.

TATE: I think you'll regret that decision, Dory.

TATE tees up her ball.

MARGOT: No, she won't. You're doing the right thing, Dory. You've got six kids and a husband you love. That's enough. Don't get greedy. Don't rock that boat.

TATE: Even if she's not happy?

MARGOT: Tough. Think about the happiness of those seven people. Seven people who love you? You've got it good. Better than most.

TATE: What do you think, Connie?

CONNIE: About having seven people love you? Sounds like under-achieving to me.

TATE hits her ball.

In the trees. Here we go again.

TATE: Well, I would hate to see you make that sacrifice and then be miserable.

MARGOT: Like you?

TATE: No, I didn't say I was miserable. I'm actually quite happy. I just don't know what the next chapter of my life will hold.

CONNIE: I do.

TATE: You do what?

CONNIE: I know what the next chapter of your life will hold.

MARGOT: So do I.

TATE: Really? And how do you know that?

MARGOT: Should we tell her?

CONNIE: I think we'd better before one of us busts.

MARGOT: Connie and I are going to back you.

TATE: Back me in what?

MARGOT: Tête-à-Tate.

CONNIE: Are you sure about that name? What about Connie's Eatery?

TATE: What are you saying?

MARGOT: Connie and I are going to be your investors. Your angels. Whatever they call them. We're going to help you get that café started.

TATE: You are?

MARGOT: Yes. So, start looking for a location.

TATE: Wait, no. I can't do that. I can't take money from friends. That is a very bad idea.

CONNIE: Oh, don't worry. This isn't a handout. We expect you to pay it back.

MARGOT: In fact, we want to be partners.

TATE: Partners?

MARGOT: Not majority shareholders, but we want a piece of the action. You manage the operation and we'll be the silent partners.

TATE: Really?

MARGOT: Really.

TATE: And you won't want to have any say in the day-to-day operation? That's all up to me?

MARGOT: All up to you.

CONNIE: Except for the name. How about Connie's Cantina?

MARGOT: The name is fine. So, what do you think, Tate? Have we got a deal?

TATE: Well, let me see if I understand this. You want me to do all the work, and you two will reap the profits?

MARGOT: Yes.

CONNIE: Exactly.

Beat.

TATE: You are the two best friends a girl could have.

TATE hugs MARGOT.

Thanks, Connie.

TATE hugs CONNIE.

CONNIE: You're welcome.

DORY: Congratulations, Tate.

TATE: Thanks, Dory.

MARGOT: Oh, and you have to curtail the drinking. Save it for after-hours when you're home with the family.

CONNIE: Yeah, let them see the dark side of you. Not us.

TATE: Don't worry. That will not be a concern from this moment on. God, I can't believe this. I think I'm going to cry.

DORY: I wonder . . .

MARGOT: What?

DORY: Well . . . could I get in on this? It might give me an excuse to visit once in a while. You know? Check up on my investment?

MARGOT: You want to invest in the café too?

DORY: If you'll have me. I mean, it would be an outlet for me. It might do me good.

MARGOT: Well . . .

TATE: No.

MARGOT: What?

TATE: No. I'm sorry, but we don't know you all that well, Dory, and you've got a history of bad money management with the gambling problem, and you're living in an unstable environment up there in the wilderness where you're not even sure about where your own life is headed, and you want us to make you a partner in a fledgling business? No. That dog won't hunt, sister. But to show you there's no hard feelings, you can have free coffee and dessert at Tête-à-Tate for life. But just you. Not your whole damn family.

TATE exits, followed by DORY.

MARGOT: *(to* CONNIE*)* I think we've hired the right manager.

MARGOT exits.

CONNIE: How about Connie's Caffeine Corral!

CONNIE exits.

THE EIGHTEENTH TEE

MARGOT, TATE, and DORY enter. They stare down the fairway.

DORY: Wow.

MARGOT: Yeah. Wow.

DORY: Look at that.

CONNIE enters.

CONNIE: That's right, ladies. Take a good, long look. Number eighteen. The final hole. Five hundred and three yards of par five hell on earth. Thick uncharted rough on both sides. Water at one hundred and eighty yards. Just close enough to tempt you into thinking you can carry it and far enough away to break the back of even the strongest-willed among us. And beyond the water, sand. That's right! So much sand that you'll think you're Lawrence of Arabia. And with a cry of "come on then!" you'll make your way to the green. A green so expansive, so undulating, that it causes the mighty to weep. Look at it. Look! And listen to what I say.

One by one, the others begin humming "The Battle Hymn of the Republic" under CONNIE's speech.

We won't all make it; I assure you of that. One or two of us will fall, struck down by the sheer magnitude and grandeur of the hole. But those that remain will snatch the standard from the fallen and will carry on in your stead, refusing to be vanquished. And if you have no stomach for this fight, then speak now, and your departure will be forgiven, for there is no shame in standing down from this most daunting task. But to those brave souls who will stay and fight this hole by my side on this day, to you I say: I hope you saved your mulligans.

MARGOT, TATE, and DORY sing the last line of the song: "His truth is marching on."

All right, the score is all tied. How exciting.

CONNIE tees up her ball.

TATE: I wonder what will happen to the money.

MARGOT: What money?

TATE: Catherine's money. She won that half a million five years ago. I wonder who it will go to.

DORY: I still can't believe she didn't tell me about that.

CONNIE: Yeah, I know if I had a gambling addict friend, she'd be the first one I'd tell about my windfall.

CONNIE hits.

Oooh, yes. That's in play.

MARGOT: I guess the money will go to her family. Her mother. Her father. Maybe her brother, Ben.

CONNIE: I should give him a call.

TATE tees up her ball.

TATE: Maybe she willed it to a charity.

MARGOT: If she had a will. I mean, she was only forty-eight. Who thinks about dying at that age? Do you think about dying?

TATE: I'm not forty-eight. I'm not anywhere close to forty-eight.

MARGOT: No?

TATE: No. I'm forty-two.

MARGOT: Really?

TATE: You don't believe me?

CONNIE: I believe her. Nobody ever lies on a golf course.

TATE hits her ball.

DORY: Maybe there was someone else besides family she would leave it to.

DORY tees up her ball.

MARGOT: Like who?

DORY: I don't know. A close friend.

MARGOT: We were her closest friends.

DORY: Then maybe you'll get it.

TATE: No.

MARGOT: I wouldn't want it. That wouldn't feel right. I mean, it's okay to inherit money from a wealthy aunt or from your parents, but not from a friend. I couldn't spend a friend's money and not feel morbid about it.

DORY hits her ball.

CONNIE: It'll probably go to her family.

MARGOT tees up her ball.

MARGOT: I hope so.

TATE: Why do you think Catherine never found anyone? A man.

CONNIE: Hard to say.

MARGOT: I don't really think she made much of an effort. She didn't go out much. She didn't put herself in a position to meet men, if you ask me.

TATE: Maybe she had the romantic notion that the right man would just show up out of nowhere one day and sweep her off her feet.

CONNIE: You mean like those princesses?

TATE: Yes. Just like that.

MARGOT hits her ball.

MARGOT: Well, she never talked to me about needing a man, so maybe it just wasn't a priority in her life.

CONNIE: Or maybe she was very particular and never found a man who measured up.

TATE: Or maybe she was quite content to be on her own.

DORY: Or maybe she was gay.

CONNIE: Yeah, right.

MARGOT: Yeah, that's a good one.

DORY: She *was* gay.

MARGOT: What?

DORY: Cathy was gay.

CONNIE: What are you talking about?

DORY: Cathy was gay. She told me a long time ago.

TATE: Are you being serious here?

DORY: Yes.

TATE: Catherine was gay?

DORY: Yes.

TATE: A lesbian.

DORY: Correct.

TATE: A homosexual.

CONNIE: All right, Tate. I think you've driven the point home.

MARGOT: You're sure about this?

DORY: She was afraid to tell you three because she didn't think you would understand.

MARGOT: And yet she told you?

TATE gasps.

TATE: Were you her lover? Partner? Boyfriend? What did we decide on?

DORY: No, I wasn't her lover.

CONNIE: I don't believe you. There's no way Catherine was gay.

DORY: She was, Connie.

CONNIE: Then why did she tell you and not us?

DORY: Because I'm four hundred miles away and a good listener. It was safe to tell me. Besides, five years ago she started bringing her girlfriend up to Arrowhead with her. That's when she told me.

MARGOT: Girlfriend?

TATE: No, I think "girlfriend" works fine in a lesbian relationship.

MARGOT: I wasn't talking about the term! She had a girlfriend?

DORY: A fellow teacher. That's another reason why she didn't tell anyone down here. She thought their jobs might be in jeopardy if the school board found out.

CONNIE: What's the other teacher's name?

DORY: That's not for me to say. And Cathy wasn't alone at the fair that night. She was with this other woman. She was on the Ferris wheel alone because the other woman is afraid of heights.

MARGOT: How do you know all this?

DORY: I've spoken to the girlfriend since Cathy's death.

TATE: I can't believe this. How could we not have known? What kind of friends are we? What about Gregory Peck?

MARGOT: What?

TATE: Catherine had a thing for Gregory Peck. Explain that.

MARGOT: Maybe she liked his acting.

Beat.

TATE: And that explains that.

CONNIE: *(to DORY)* So, if Catherine didn't want us to know, what makes you think you have the right to tell us her secret now? After she's gone.

DORY: She had finally made the decision to tell you. She felt bad about hiding it from you all these years. Bad for you and bad for her. She wrote me a letter last week and told me.

She takes out a letter and hands it to CONNIE.

I wasn't going to tell you but you were all so damned oblivious and stupid and ill-informed about your best friend that you drove me to it. And Tate, you're right. How could you not have known? What kind of friends are you?

DORY exits.

CONNIE: She wasn't lying. It's all here in the letter.

TATE: I feel horrible.

MARGOT: Why? What have you got to feel horrible about?

TATE: Well, that our friend didn't feel she could tell us something like that. Something that important to her.

MARGOT: That's not our fault. I'm not going to take the blame for that. We came out here every week for fourteen years. You mean to tell me there wasn't one time when she felt she could open up to us? Not one opportunity? No. In fact, I feel betrayed. With all the things that we shared with her over the years? My daughter. My marriage breakup. And the grocery list of problems that you two carry around. And she hid this from us? No. She's the one who should feel horrible. Not us.

MARGOT exits.

TATE: She wants a dead woman to feel horrible?

CONNIE: Yeah. Overkill, huh? And what's this about a grocery list of problems? What's that about?

TATE: Beats me.

CONNIE: What problems do we have?

TATE: None. Except for your promiscuity.

CONNIE: And your lousy sex life.

TATE: And your narcissism.

CONNIE: And that lazy-eyed kid of yours.

They exit.

THE NINETEENTH TEE

DORY enters first, followed by MARGOT and TATE.

DORY: No, listen, I shouldn't have said that, and I'm sorry. My emotions got the better of me. I had no right calling you oblivious and ill-informed.

TATE: You called us stupid too.

DORY: Yeah.

MARGOT: And I had no right saying what I said, Tate. I did feel betrayed, but Catherine must have had a reason for not telling us. Maybe we did make her feel like she couldn't tell us, and if so, I regret that. I'm very sad about that.

TATE: That's all right, Margot. It's an emotional time. We're all feeling a little sad right now.

CONNIE enters marking the scorecard.

CONNIE: And we win! Yes! Boom shakalakalaka! Boom shaka-lakalaka! So, where are you losers taking us for lunch?

MARGOT: Actually, can we take you to lunch another time?

CONNIE: What? No. Dory's going home tomorrow.

MARGOT: Well, I would like to go and call my daughter. I'm worried that maybe I haven't given her a chance to say some things to me, the way I didn't with Catherine.

TATE: You think your daughter is gay?

MARGOT: No, Tate. I just think that we should talk.

CONNIE: So, call her after lunch. You haven't spoken in two years. What's two more hours?

MARGOT: I'm glad to see you're working on that insensitivity problem you have.

DORY: I'll buy you lunch, Connie. And you too, Tate. I don't want to have any outstanding gambling debts.

TATE: No, I've got a better idea. You can buy us lunch the next time you're in town. It'll give you an excuse to get away from Arrowhead Lake for a while. How does that sound?

DORY: That sounds perfect.

TATE: And who knows, maybe we'll be lunching at Tête-à-Tate.

DORY: I'd love that.

MARGOT: Well, I guess this is it then.

DORY: Yeah, I guess it is.

MARGOT: It was nice meeting you, Dory.

DORY: Thanks Margot. You too.

MARGOT and DORY hug.

MARGOT: Have a safe trip back tomorrow.

DORY: I will.

TATE: I wish you all the best up there, Dory.

DORY: Thanks, Tate.

TATE and DORY hug. DORY then turns to CONNIE.

TATE: And don't forget, you've got free coffee and dessert for life at my café.

DORY: Right. But just me. Not my whole damn family.

TATE: Right.

DORY turns to CONNIE and opens her arms.

DORY: Connie?

CONNIE: I'm more of a handshake person.

CONNIE and DORY shake hands.

Nice meeting you. You play a good game of golf.

DORY: Thank you. Coming from you, that means absolutely nothing.

CONNIE: Hey, the woman's got spunk. I like that.

TATE: *(near tears)* Oh, God.

MARGOT: Tate, what's wrong now?

TATE: I just realized that this was the last place I saw Catherine. Last week. On this very spot. We said goodbye, and I said, "See you next week." She gave a little wave and a smile, and she was gone.

MARGOT: It was the last time I saw her too.

CONNIE: Me too.

TATE: Maybe this was where we should have said some words for her. Maybe she would have heard them from here.

MARGOT: Well . . . we could say some now.

DORY: That's a good idea.

TATE: Okay. But what kind of words? Should it be a prayer or just something nice and sweet?

MARGOT: I don't know. Connie? You're the broadcaster.

CONNIE: I broadcast the news. I don't broadcast benedictions.

TATE: Would we bow our heads?

MARGOT: If you want to.

TATE: Then I would definitely take off my visor because bowing your head is like praying.

CONNIE: I'm not praying.

MARGOT: Why not?

CONNIE: Because God wouldn't buy it. God knows me too well.

TATE: So it won't be a prayer?

CONNIE: It won't be a prayer.

TATE: Then I'll leave my visor on.

CONNIE: So, who's going to say it?

MARGOT: I'll say it.

TATE: No. We don't need a repeat of the whole "you went to the fair and now you're dead" thing.

MARGOT: Well, you won't say it.

TATE: I'd be no good at it.

MARGOT: You see?

CONNIE: Oh, let's forget it then.

TATE: Why?

CONNIE: Because we don't know what to say and we can't decide who will say it. It'll be a fiasco. It won't be a fitting tribute at all.

MARGOT: She's right.

CONNIE: Of course I'm right. Tate? Agreed?

Beat.

TATE: I suppose.

CONNIE: Good. Now, let's go.

MARGOT, TATE, and CONNIE begin to leave. DORY starts to sing.

DORY: "The water is wide. I can't cross o'er.
And neither have I wings to fly.
Give me a boat that can carry two,
And both shall row, my love and I.

The others join in.

ALL: There is a ship, and she sails the sea.
She's loaded deep as deep can be.
But not so deep as the love I'm in;
I know not how I sink or swim.

I know not how I sink or swim."

Lights down.

End.

After twenty-five years in radio arts, Norm Foster dis-covered the world of theatre and began his legacy as Canada's most-produced playwright. He has penned an impressive array of plays, including a handful of musicals, that have been produced across North America. Norm lives in Fredericton, New Brunswick.

First edition: September 2015. Second printing: February 2019.
Printed and bound in Canada by Imprimerie Gauvin, Gatineau

Cover design and illustration by Patrick Gray

**PLAYWRIGHTS
CANADA PRESS**

202-269 Richmond St. W.
Toronto, ON
M5V 1X1

416.703.0013
info@playwrightscanada.com
playwrightscanada.com
@playcanpress